VALUES, ETHICS
AND AGING

VALUES, ETHICS AND AGING

Edited by

Gari Lesnoff-Caravaglia, Ph.D.

University of Massachusetts Center on Aging
Worcester, Massachusetts

Volume IV, Frontiers in Aging Series
Series Editor: Gari Lesnoff-Caravaglia, Ph.D.

 **HUMAN SCIENCES PRESS, INC.**
72 FIFTH AVENUE
NEW YORK, N.Y. 10011

Printed in the United States of America
123456789

Library of Congress Cataloging in Publication Data
Main entry under title:

Values, ethics, and aging.

  (Frontiers in aging series, ISSN 0271-955X; v. 4)

  Includes index.
  1. Aged—Social conditions—Addresses, essays, lectures. 2.
Aged—Religious life—Addresses, essays, lectures. 3. Aged—Services
for—Addresses, essays, lectures. 4. Social ethics—Addresses, essays,
lectures. 5. Social role—Addresses, essays, lectures.
I. Lesnoff-Caravaglia, Gari. II. Series.

HQ1061.V34   305.2'6   83-22627
ISBN 0-89885-162-9

DEDICATED TO

Professor George F. Kneller, for leading me to appreciate the
relationship between philosophy and existence.

CONTENTS

7

CONTRIBUTORS

W. Andrew Achenbaum, Ph.D., Assistant Professor, Department of History and Philosophy, Carnegie-Mellon University, Pittsburgh, Pennsylvania

George J. Alexander, J.S.D., Dean, School of Law, University of Santa Clara, Santa Clara, California

Virginia Lee Boyack, Ph.D., The Life Planning Office, California Federal Savings, Los Angeles, California

Lydia Bragger, The Gray Panthers, New York, New York

Donald F. Clingan, D. Min., Executive Director, National Center on Ministry With the Aging, Indianapolis, Indiana

Thomas C. Cook, Jr., M.Div., Executive Director, National Interfaith Coalition on Aging, Athens, Georgia

G. Cullom Davis, Ph.D., Professor of History; Director, Oral History Office, Sangamon State University, Springfield, Illinois

Jerome Kaplan, Ph.D., Executive Director, Mansfield Memorial Homes; Adjunct Professor of Sociology, Ohio State University, Mansfield, Ohio

Margaret J. Kustaborder, M.N., Clinical Nurse Specialist, St. John's North, Springfield, Illinois

Gerald A. Larue, Th.D., Professor of Biblical History and Archaeology, School of Religion, University of Southern California, Los Angeles, California

Gari Lesnoff-Caravaglia, Ph.D., Executive Director, University Center on Aging; Professor, Family and Community Medicine, University of Massachusetts Medical Center, Worcester, Massachusetts

Harry R. Moody, Ph.D., Brookdale Center on Aging, Hunter College, New York, New York

Harold M. Stahmer, Ph.D., Professor of Religion and Philosophy; Associate Director, Center for Gerontological Studies and Programs, University of Florida, Gainesville, Florida

Carleton J. Sweetser, M.Div., Chaplain and Director, Department of Religious Services, St. Luke's Roosevelt Hospital Center, New York, New York

PREFACE

This is a time when more of the world's population are sharing the experience of aging and old age than ever before in the history of the globe, and we are looking forward to a period when even greater numbers of people will enjoy or suffer many years of life beyond the age of 65. This is not an American phenomenon, it is world-wide; and so are the predicted and immediate general and particular crises and problems associated with old age, from the crises over Social Security and Medicare and the threat of a generational conflict, to the increasing literature of advice addressed to, if not read by, younger people about how one goes about growing old gracefully, successfully, painlessly, and imperceptibly. Why the anxiety, the sudden concern since, as many people have observed, men and women have grown old since time out of mind, and since societies and individuals seem to have managed to deal with these so-called problems one way or another? All of this is true, and yet in the past there was very little individual and collective attention to growing old. The visible elders in society held positions of power and status, and age generally was associated with respect. Those individuals who suffered disabilities in old age did not fare well, and one way or another they dropped out of society un-noticed—the invisible old.

It is indeed the large number of people who are now counted among the old by society, and the rapidly increasing number that we expect to live into their late 70s and 80s that has focused attention on the problems and the process during the last three decades. These people are being heard and noticed in a variety of ways as never be-fore. Some social workers, a few government statisticians, one or two physicians and economists early in the 20th century discovered that the number of people over 65 was increasing at a more rapid rate than the population as a whole, and that their problems concerned or should concern the whole society. It wasn't, however, until after World War II that the interdisciplinary specialization of gerontology was established, made up primarily of social scientists, with some biologists and clini-cians. And it wasn't until the early 70s that humanists began to discover old age and aging as an important and shared human experience.

This collection of essays demonstrates not only that the disciplines of the humanities may add significantly to the understanding of the psychological and social aspects of aging but that humanists, using the skills and content of their disciplines, can add an all-important di-mension to programs for improving the quality of life of the elderly. This volume should find a distinguished place on the small but grow-ing shelf of books in the humanities on aging.

David D. Van Tassel, Ph.D.
Case Western Reserve University
Cleveland, Ohio

Chapter 1

THE AESTHETIC ATTITUDE AND COMMON EXPERIENCE

Gari Lesnoff-Caravaglia

The aesthetic attitude—the appreciation and enjoyment of beauty—is not a closed esoteric term, but rather a concept which pervades all of life and calls forth a reaction from young and old, infirm and healthy, as well as the dying. The aesthetic attitude forms the basis for many of our choices in life and the many decisions which influence the pattern of our lives. It might be called the common denominator of human experiencing.

Whether in the selection of friends or companions, the decoration of our homes, the purchase of a garment, the preparation of a dinner menu, participation in a ritual or ceremony or holiday celebration, we find the aesthetic attitude comes into play. Much of social participation has this aesthetic expression at its core.

We react to other personalities, to the appearance of persons, to their social attributes, on the basis of aesthetics. We use expressions which clearly indicate such criteria. For example: "I would not be seen with him!" or, "She is not my type." A common observation is: "Can you imagine marrying *her*? What does he *see* in her?" In other words, she offends my aesthetic sense or taste.

The aesthetic attitude is also closely tied to the concept of self.

We find this expressed in remarks such as "*I* would never do or say such a thing." Or, "How could you think that *I* would want that!"

There is a dimension to aesthetics that is practical as well, such as with an efficient, smooth-handled tool. Equally pleasing is a cup that is curved to the lip and which lifts and sets easily. The gleaming sides of a powerful industrial machine also have a compelling attraction.

How the aesthetic attitude develops is difficult to assess. It is clear, however, that it is closely tied to one's self-esteem or identity, and certainly is linked to the human need freely and independently to elect a unique lifestyle. Not always, but on occasion, such an expression of self-determination may require a certain amount of financial freedom.

The aesthetic sense, however, if unnourished or unsupported, much like other human capabilities, can be thwarted or frustrated—if not extinguished. Such unfortunately is the case for many older persons who are forced to live their lives by minimal standards imposed upon them by an impersonal authority. Such restriction is also to be found in diminished opportunities in education, work, socialization, travel, and general participation on an equal footing with other age groups in the mainstream of life. The most serious restriction of all, of course, is financial. In effect, what the imposition of minimal standards does is to ask older persons to alter their sense of identity.

The loss continuum which we describe as part of the aging process, the loss in such areas as health, sensory capacities, changes in role, retirement, and death, ought really to include the loss of aesthetic expression as well. Such loss is evident in the most ordinary of human experience.

Food is an excellent example. Food is central to human behavior, and it is not surprising that the partaking of food forms part of many rites and rituals. Food and love are almost synonymous symbolically. We use food as a symbol of love when we prepare a favorite dish for a favored person. Large meals crown family reunions and are the hallmark of holidays we enjoy the most, such as Thanksgiving, Christmas, and Easter. Holiday pleasure is largely due to the sharing of such a meal with other persons. In fact, when family members are not able to be present at holiday time, it is not at all unusual to invite other persons to share in this meal. The sharing in itself has significance.

If we examine the role of food closely, we begin to see that much of what we refer to as aesthetics is directly related to the preparation and enjoyment of food. To begin with, eating is a social event—we seldom prepare a large meal to eat alone. The preparation of a meal subsumes the notion of other people.

The ingestion of food is also related to psychological states. People who are depressed are often not interested in eating. Similarly, older persons who live alone frequently do not eat properly, and there arises what we call the tea and toast syndrome. For people alone, the preparation of a meal may consist solely of frozen dinners or snack food which have little nutritional value.

Eating is part of what we expect when we plan a festivity. A good dinner precedes going to the theatre or concert. Following a cultural event, it is customary to stop for something to eat. The supper heightens the conviviality of the occasion and adds an aesthetic dimension to the total experience.

When we meet a friend we have not seen for some time, an expression of our pleasure is to invite the friend to dinner. When a person is experiencing a temporary setback, it is not unusual to suggest a cup of tea. For the British and the Russians, tea is a veritable panacea for all ills.

Furthermore, we have set aside a room for just this purpose. The table is set, decorated, and the seating of persons around the table has some importance in ensuring that a pleasant and agreeable table companion accompanies the repast.

All of this has little to do with naked hunger and the need to fuel up the machine so that it can continue to operate efficiently. The picture is much more complex.

There are now a number of facilities providing noonday meals to older persons. The environment in which many such nutrition sites are located frequently leave much to be desired from the standpoint of aesthetics.

Bearing in mind the importance of setting, preparation, and circumstances surrounding the eating of food, I should like to describe what happens at some nutrition sites. There is generally a serving line, with persons selecting paper napkins and plastic utensils before reaching the food counter. There the food is ladled out onto paper plates and handed over the counter to the waiting individual. When food must be directly handled by the server, the hand that reaches out to the person's plate is covered with plastic. The diner does not serve him or herself in any way.

As I moved through the line on one occasion, a small, frail-looking woman preceded me. I started to take a piece of bread off the serving plate with my hand, when a plastic hand swiftly countered my move by dropping two slices of white bread on my paper plate. The woman in front of me looked at me with a smile.

"I know it looks odd to be served by that plastic hand. It reminds me of the way they handle radioactive substances. I know it is to make sure the food is germfree, but I sometimes get the feeling that it is not my food they are protecting, but themselves."

I looked at her quizzically, and she continued. "I feel as though it is the plate of an old person they don't wish to touch. . ." She smiled painfully, and added in an undertone, "We are the untouchables."

People passed from the serving line to sit at tables where they ate quickly, without speaking to the persons sitting nearby.

Another example is that of a site in which the diners apparently took some initiative in determining what a dining area should be like. At this location, in the center of the room was a large table covered with a lace tablecloth on which was arranged a bouquet of flowers. Several plates of carrot and celery sticks and the like were set out. People entering would stop to nibble on the raw vegetables while they chatted and waited for the serving line to open. The tablecloth, flowers, and vegetables were provided by the diners. Following the meal, coffee was served in the adjoining room where the card tables were being set up. People joined in clearing the dining table. The combination of eating and sociability was very real. People smiled and chatted in an animated fashion.

I was there that day to conduct a workshop entitled *Leadership Training for Older Adults*. I felt I had much to learn from that particular group.

Still a third example: this was a nutrition site for elderly Chinese. The setting was the second floor of a large Chinese restaurant. Persons as they entered moved to sit with what appeared to be groups of friends. Others, as they stood hesitantly, wondering where to sit, were nodded to a place by someone already seated at a table. In the center of the tables were large lazy susans.

The program was initiated by the director of the nutrition site introducing a woman from the Heart Association, who presented a program on health, flanked on both sides by huge posters illustrating the heart and possible problems. The audience listened politely. Following this presentation, the director turned the program over to an older woman. She delivered an address in Chinese which seemed to consist primarily of announcements; she then introduced a small wiry gentleman who was seated at a nearby table. As he stood up, the applause was resounding, smiles broke out on all faces, and people nodded to one another in pleasurable anticipation. The gentleman began what seemed to be a story, enacted in pantomime and gestures which had the audience in stitches. The story clearly dealt with a young woman and her unwelcome suitor, and finally culminated in a duel with swords, all conveyed in pantomime. It was amazingly easy to follow. He finished his tale to thunderous applause.

The meal was then placed on the lazy susans at each table, and people served themselves and one another. One marvelous old woman kept filling my cup with tea. The Chinese food was exceptionally good. As the meal was drawing to a close, another woman got up from one of the tables and began to sing; the rest of the people chimed in during the refrain. At the end of the song there was more applause, and the people filed out of the dining room. The director stood at the door and returned their bows and smiles.

What does all of this have to do with aesthetic attitude? Everything.

The aesthetic sense is, of course, closely related to the arts, but not exclusively. In a very real sense, one can speak of art and human welfare—or of the healing role of the arts. Artistic expression has always been part of folk culture and religion in earliest human history. The ancient use of the arts was therapeutic as well as a form of aesthetic expression. The ancients did not deny, but indeed stressed the fact that the arts are a necessary component in any individual life, crucial to personal expression and well-being.

The enjoyment of the arts is thus a basic human need, equal to the need for food, shelter, and clothing. The arts are not a frill, something nice but unnecessary, and aesthetics is an integral part of daily experiencing.

Formerly, art was found predominantly in the church. Religious sculpture as well as the tombs in the cemeteries bear witness to this practical expression of aesthetic need. Homes were built to endure, and frescoes, paintings on the walls and ceilings, were a further

testimony to this sense of permanence through time for human enjoyment. A fresco painting like *The Death of Adam* by Piero della
Francesca in Arezzo was for generations to enjoy. Religious art was
not esoteric, but meant for universal consumption.

Art was expected to play a part in the overall harmony of human
existence from birth through death. Art thus was spiritual in the sense
that it also had as its goal the transcending of daily experiencing on a
routine level.

Art led to an awareness that was outside of ordinary living and
led to the creation of forms which communicated intimacy—intimate
feeling—and compensated for internal and external chaos. It was a
way of transcending the self, if only for brief moments. The world, or
one's personal experience of the world, might appear as without
meaning or goal, but such aesthetic harmony enabled one to perceive
a pattern which restored meaning to life.

It appears that the aesthetic sense is greatly heightened or
escalates in moments of crisis. For example, the song of a bird is
never so poignant as at the moment of despair, or the pattern of a leaf
against a wall more graphic than at a time of anguish, such as major
illness. Moments of crisis are etched in memory through human emotion and such intensified perception. Poetry which catches such feeling, like that of Emily Dickinson, recognizes such acuity at the pitch
of human passion.

The lives of many older persons can well be described as lives in
crisis. A perpetual crisis is created by separation from families,
removal from familiar environments, limitation in freedom and
decision-making, as well as the changes in health status and the subtle, gradual loss of the senses of hearing and sight. Such crises are
cumulative in effect. Even moments of despair separated in time run
into one another and can be overwhelming in effect. One example is
the dying of relatives and friends within a short period of time. Relief,
by way of the arts, is not to be slighted.

The need for aesthetic expression may be keenest in dire circumstances. In concentration camps, for example, the rare recreational programs such as art lessons or theatricals were what saved persons from total personal annihilation and helped to preserve their personal dignity. Such persons have reported that they would have gone
without their meager rations rather than forego the opportunity for
such expression of feeling.

Environments of crisis are all around us. The hospital, prison, and nursing home are but a few examples. The heightened reception of sensory stimuli due to a crisis setting is magnified by the bleak and impersonal aspect of many of these institutions. Paradoxically, the aesthetic sense is quickened by an impoverished environment—almost as a form of survival arousal. The appreciation of life is best understood by those who have had a close brush with death. Reading the accounts of persons who have experienced heart transplants or similar radical surgery gives some indication of the intensified appreciation of sound, color, light, and human interaction.

The fact that nursing homes have adopted the hospital model is partly due to the ease of replicating a sterile environment. What is currently referred to as the hospital model is questionable as an environment suitable for health care at any age; the lack of stimuli alone makes it a deprived and depriving environment.

We have recognized the need for stimulating environments for children. Even intensive care nurseries provide toys, colorful window shades, and nurses in uniforms of pastel colors.

The separation of creativity and aesthetic appreciation from the everyday experiencing of life is done consciously. It is only on the unconscious level that we incorporate such needs into the fabric of our lives. The culture militates against such open expression. Thus our concept of art, along with the concept of aging, is myth-ridden. Both share a common negative connotation.

Artistic creation or an interest in the arts is popularly regarded as a weakness or a form of effeminate behavior. Art appears to be appropriately indulged in if you are well-to-do, particularly if you seem to manifest such interest as a form of duty. This may well have roots in one historical tradition that regarded the pursuit of the arts as a proper activity for the leisure class which was at a loss as to how to pass the time. From this historical perspective and unfortunately into the present day, art is for those for whom the provision of the basic necessities of life is not a problem.

Once the lower-level biological and physiological needs are satisfied, then we can move on to the higher, more sublime needs. Our tendency to explain human behavior through the formation of such hierarchies has hampered our ability to understand human qualities of being. One clear example is our adherence to levels of need, progressing from one so-called basic level and then moving up to another, until we reach the least basic—possibly the aesthetic. Such a scheme is very reminiscent of the stages of dying through which persons are assumed to move until the final moment. Such models may have some didactic validity, however limited, but they invalidly presume to describe the complexity of human experiencing. Perceptions and reactions in living are far too complex and individual for such simplistic diagramming.

Art is further regarded as an activity to be engaged in by those with specific talents or skills. Creative activity is frequently considered as something to be provided for young, developing persons. Art for older individuals has usually been viewed as in the nature of "crafts"—the doing over of old castaway items into something else equally useless: behavior which somehow subtly reflects the negative stereotyping of older persons themselves. Such misconceptions with respect to art and aging have led to their mutual impoverishment.

Art can improve mental and physical functioning and can even prolong life. Older persons have needs which go beyond the realm of health care alone. What it means to grow old in emotional terms, or in terms of personal feeling, has yet to be fully explored. Art can be part of general health maintenance and prevention and can offset the meaninglessness which induces depression and, subsequently, ill health.

When the world of the older person shrinks (as it does for many), undue emphasis is often placed upon physical and material needs. There is an artificial separation of physical self from the aesthetic, emotional, or spiritual. Physical care takes precedence, and often is the only consideration given the older individual. Participation in the various art forms can without question expand the personal horizons of older persons and offer them a sense of continuity and a healthy feeling of belonging. Personal well-being, both mental and physical, frequently relies upon a sense of continued participation in the wider world.

An older individual who can express his or her past through a creative form, in a healthy sense integrates past experience into present functioning. For example, an elderly Sicilian who spent the greater portion of his adult life in an Eastern industrial city, when forced to retire, began to paint scenes from his childhood in Sicily. He focused primarily upon his religious education, and processions and church scenes populated any kind of rudimentary canvas he could find. One large section of poster board was devoted to the facade of the village church. His real artistic triumph, however, took the form of a small chapel, complete with stone fountain devoted to the Virgin Mary, which he built with pebbles collected from the neighborhood and local beach. He located the chapel at the end of his driveway, in full view of passersby. It was not long before the local press featured the chapel as an ingenious work of art, and grandchildren and children gathered at his home to admire and praise his handiwork. The elderly gentleman took obvious pride in his work and it was a triumph of transcendence over nostalgia and reminiscence. He had continued to develop as an individual and he used his past remembrance to impart meaning to his present life.

Involvement in the arts may well become the medical prescription of the future. Just as physicians today instruct pre-coronary patients to alter their diets, to relax, or to slacken their work schedules, physicians of tomorrow may prescribe music, dance, or the introspective exercise of poetic creation.

This is not a new discovery. People constantly cope with their world by translating deep feeling into art. Welsh miners emerge singing from the earth; work songs such as *The Erie Canal* and *I'm a-working on the railroad*, which now form the repertoire of folk singers, were part of the aesthetic expression of laborers. *The Volga Boatman* is unmistakably sung to the rhythmic washing of the oars through the water. The spirituals also were an expression of faith and frustration. We continue to enjoy sacred music for particular religious occasions; strong contrasts are presented between the music to celebrate a death and that to celebrate a wedding.

As a further example, dance was once the sacred language the shaman used to communicate with the vast unknown. In prehistoric times, the shaman was both priest and physician. Only with the rise of Western civilization were the body and mind conceived of as distinctly separate. Doctor and priest were seen as separate professions. It was then that the dance was viewed as different from the arts of healing, and came to be thought of as frivolous and superficial.

Painting, musical composition, drawing, dance, and theatre are all special languages for expressing the world as it is experienced. They can also be used to comment upon the world and to criticize. It comes as no surprise to us when productive persons of talent are rejected in their native lands when they turn their pen or brush to criticize society as they know it.

The opportunity for older individuals to participate in the art world depends not only upon their own resources, capabilities, interests, and aspiration, but derives to a larger extent from the perception of older persons by the art world and the general public. When viewed negatively, older persons are given limited or little access to the arts and art education.

When opportunities do exist, we find that participation in the arts and art education can provide older persons with avenues for self-expression which can open up new vistas of achievement, new roles, and new interests. All these serve to compensate, at times, for some of the social, physical, and economic losses many older persons experience. For through the arts one transcends the present and participates on a highly personal level in a timeless moment. It is an absorption that permits of no conventional accounting of time. Such intense intellectual activity is true of the scientist, the mathematician, as it is of the ceramist, the weaver, the sculptor, or composer. Anyone who sews knows what such absorption means. Reading a good novel is on the same level of experience.

The arts can also increase the human repertoire for dealing with new situations, with transitions from one life-experience to another, with frustrations, and for the building of new reservoirs of self-esteem, new relationships, and interests. The ability to respond to life on a variety of levels, within a range of dimensions, is something participation in the arts can insure. Such increased awareness of self, the world, and of other human beings, comes through sensitivity to sound, light, color, and rhythm.

The renewal of self through participation in the arts is not a new concept. This forms the basis of much of our therapeutic activity. That such capacity for renewal is requisite to remaining a functioning and experiencing human being, throughout the lifespan, has yet to be recognized. Studies of creativity, like curves of intelligence, do not indicate sharp drops as we grow older. Creative activity and intellectual ability alike reach a point of development, and then level off. They both drop significantly only in advanced old age, and then usually only at the onset of serious illness.

What can be done? We can begin by encouraging various agencies on the local, state, and national level to take a major role in developing collaborative opportunities so that councils on the arts and the networks of services for older persons can be supportive and life-enhancing.

We can encourage practitioners, persons working with and for older persons, to become active advocates for older persons and the arts. Professional artists need to be educated to the artistic needs and interests of our rapidly aging nation. With the expectation of longer life, the quality of experience lies in artistic expression and aesthetic appreciation.

Further, special supports and opportunities are needed, not solely because of the disabilities of old age, but principally to offset the negative stereotyping of older individuals which allows them to be seen as dull, apathetic, uninterested, and uninteresting.

One of the original intentions of the arts was to point to problems and paradoxes to be found within society. The arts served a critical function. It may well be that increasing involvement of older persons in the arts will sharpen this focus of the arts once again and make them more lively and meaningful.

Theatre, dance, painting, writing, need not always have professionalism as their ultimate goal. Equally legitimate is the goal of self-expression, with creativity seen as a value in itself. This is a concept of creativity which is stressed from kindergarden to grade 12, and then stressed no more.

The role of play in society as fundamental to well-being has virtually disappeared. We are all so busy hurrying through the educational process, then on to the task of earning a living, and then fulfilling our duties as family members, that only belatedly do we realize that we have been hurrying toward oblivion. We have trivialized existence. Trivia has supplanted the living of life: the trivia of routine, social obligation, fear of censure or criticism if we depart from the usual or expected. We both admire and fear an authentic individual.

Teachers of persons of all age levels, in informal instruction as well as formal, need to develop a lifespan perspective. Such a perspective permits of the recognition that what is important and life-enhancing at younger ages may be equally so, if not more, at advanced ages.

Interest in developing arts for older persons is predicated upon the belief that as we grow older, we can learn to understand ourselves and other persons that much better; that we have within us the ability to teach others from the wealth of our wider knowledge and experience, if allowed and encouraged to do so. For this to occur, the proper environment must be fostered.

The point is not only to facilitate the integration of the aging into the arts, but to integrate the arts into human services. As an outcome, we should hope that public and private art and aging agencies, institutions, and organizations will encourage collaborative efforts to insure older persons maximum access to, and participation in, cultural programs and services.

For it is under the art of living that all other arts are subsumed. We need to move away from the notion that mind and body are separate, and to stop looking at what is referred to as "basic" needs as somehow antithetical to human enjoyment. The arts can play a healing role—and it is not too farfetched to suggest that the medical prescription of the future may not be limited to pills and dosages, but may direct the client toward aesthetic enjoyment or appreciation.

The advantage of being an aging nation is that it causes us to examine all of our values and ethical positions. It might also lead us to examine more closely our services—as well as disservices—to the elderly.

BIBLIOGRAPHY

Butler, R.N. The destiny of creativity in later life: Studies of creative people and the creative process. In S. Levin & R.J. Kahena, (Eds.), *Psychodynamic studies on aging: Creativity, reminiscing and dying.* New York: International Universities Press, 1967.

de Beauvoir, S. *The coming of age.* New York: G.P. Putnam, 1973.

Harris, L., & Associates. *The myth and reality of aging in America.* Washington, D.C.: National Council on the Aging, 1975.

Manney, J.D., Jr. *Aging in American society.* Ann Arbor, Michigan: Institute of Gerontology, University of Michigan, 1975.

May, R. *The courage to create.* New York: Norton, 1975.

Rockefeller Foundation. *The healing role of the arts.* New York: The Rockefeller Foundation Working Papers, July, 1978.

Spicker, S.F., Woodward, K.M. & Van Tassel, D.D. (Eds.). *Aging and the elderly.* Atlantic Highlands, New Jersey: Humanities Press, 1978.

Chapter 2

VALUES, ETHICS AND AGING

Harold M. Stahmer

In *Why Survive: Being Old in America*, Dr. Robert Butler (1975), former Director of the National Institute on Aging, observes:

> Aging is the neglected stepchild of the human life cycle. Though we have begun to examine the socially taboo subjects of dying and death, we have leaped over that long period of time preceding death known as old age. In truth, it is easier to manage the problem of death than the problem of living as an old person (p.1).

And it was either the historian Arnold Toynbee or the statesman Winston Churchill who was reported to have said that the quality of any society can be judged in terms of its treatment of and attitudes towards both its elderly and, ironically, or not surprisingly, its prison population.

While preparing this chapter I found that I kept asking myself whether or not many of our concerns about ethical questions affecting the elderly might be reduced if our social values and priorities could be changed. Shouldn't those involved with improving the quality of life for our nation's elderly be exploring or at least considering alternate social structures and economic systems? On the other hand, we can invest vast sums of the taxpayers' dollars to set up think tanks to explore strategies for dealing with the crises in Iran and Afghanistan. But seldom do we hear our nation's leaders calling for summit planning to consider an alternate economic and social system to provide a more efficient delivery system for the goods and services needed by an increasingly larger and older segment of our population. Although I do not pretend to have answers to this kind of question, it does not in any way minimize the importance of raising what I would call the larger issue of social values. Are the values, for example, inherent in the Protestant work ethic still valid? In an essay entitled *Human Values, Economic Values and the Elderly*, former Commerce Secretary Juanita Kreps (Van Tassel, 1979) discusses the social implications for the elderly of continuing to value a person's worth in "dollar terms." She states that the argument that earnings reflect productive worth says nothing about the value of the individual beyond this economic framework.

"Nevertheless," she insists, that "there is a strong tendency to equate human worth with earnings." And that, "It is this tendency that renders the elderly *valueless* to society" (p. 11).

> Indeed, by the current productivity standard a retiree merely consumes the output of others just as a child does; both must depend on others for support. The important difference between retiree and child. . .lies in their potential. Whereas investments in the young person will "pay off" because he will become a producer, spending for the older dependent yields no future return. Hence, it is easy to develop an economic rationale for heavy investments in the education of youth. But the cost of supporting the aged is not recouped, and there is some tendency to view these expenditures as poor investments (p. 12).

Dr. Kreps suggests that we humanists get involved in this kind of social questioning in two ways. "First, by insisting that productivity is not an acceptable measure of human worth, and second by specifying an alternative scheme for valuing human beings" (p. 12).

We have thought for so long in terms of *time* as precious money that we are ill-prepared to explore the implications of leisure or other forms of time either during our productive working years or as retirees. Recently, I was living in a famous German Benedictine monastery in the Rhineland studying an exchange of letters between the Jewish philosopher Martin Buber and a Benedictine monk with whom I had studied for a year after graduating from college 30 years ago. The Benedictines, who are currently celebrating the 1500 anniversary of their founder, are famous for their observance of the monastic hours which consume about a third of their working hours each day. Time is precious to them but mainly as a way of preparing themselves as spiritual creatures in this life for the life to follow. And yet how strange that critics of modern technology and capitalism like Lewis Mumford and Werner Sombart should identify the Benedictines as architects of modern capitalism. In his essay *The Monastery and the Clock* in *Technics and Civilization,* Lewis Mumford (1963) points out that the Benedictines in the thirteenth century used the clock to regularize their observance of the monastic hours throughout the more than 40,000 monasteries in Europe at that time. He states that "Coulton agrees with Sombart in looking upon the Benedictines, the great working order, as perhaps the original founders of modern capitalism." Use of the clock gradually spread outside the monastery and brought a new regularity into the life of the workman and the merchant. "The clock," argues Mumford, "not the steam engine, is the key machine of the modern industrial age" (pp. 13-14). Although clock time is not natural or native to the human experience, this abstract concept of time became a dominant factor in the ordering of our life throughout the industrialized world. We forget, for example, how alien mechanical time was and is to the human organism. As Mumford points out,

> Human life has regularities of its own, the beat of the pulse, the breathing of the lungs, these change from hour to hour with mood and action, and in the longer span of days, time is measured not by the calendar but by the events that occupy it. The shepherd measures from the time the ewes lambed, the farmer measures back to the day of sowing or forward to the harvest (p. 15).

Upon reflection, it is understandable how difficult it is for our human organisms to cope with the pressures of mechanical time during our 9 to 5, 5 day work weeks, and then be cut loose from this domination and be told as retirees to enjoy your new leisure time. In McLuhan's words, our systems may be so massaged by mechanical time that we are incapable of discovering or asserting time frequencies more attuned to our basic humanity or creatureliness. As Dr. Kreps (Van Tassel, 1979) puts it, "During working life, the constant drive to produce, to use time wisely, to increase one's position or income through extra work, pervades all we do. . .As a result of the individual's work ethic, the impact of technology that could increase productivity, and thus allow people the luxury of greater freedom from toil, is subverted" (p. 15).

A United Nations statement on *The Aging: Trends and Policies* observes:

> Strongly competitive societies in which too much emphasis is given to an individual's worth in terms of productive work and achievement, in which inactivity is somewhat suspect and leisure is highly commercialized and therefore expensive are not congenial environments in which to grow old (Van Tassel, 1979, p. 11).

Unfortunately, a survey of recent literature on future directions in our society does not suggest that we are on the threshold of ushering in major constructive or positive changes in our social values. We still are fascinated with terms like success, growth, expansion, and technology, and our appeal to and preoccupation with a youth-oriented culture seems undiminished.

When referring to "values," I use the term as defined by the sociologist Robin Williams (1970) in his classic study, *American Society*, where he notes that ". . .we here define values as those conceptions of desirable stages of affairs that are utilized in selective conduct as *criteria* for preference or choice or as *justifications* for proposed or actual behavior" (p. 442).

Given such a definition, it is not always easy to distinguish "values" from a social "ethic" as embodied, for example, in the "Protestant work ethic." One standard text on ethics (Jones et al., 1977) defines "ethics" or "an ethic" as "a pattern or norm or code of conduct actually adopted by a group of people (although, of course, not necessarily always obeyed). Ethics, like values, can be studied and defined by sociologists, philosophers, anthropologists, political theorists, and students of religion and theology, to mention but a few disciplines and approaches" (p.1ff.). Because our interests are primarily practical rather than theoretical, I hope that the experts in ethical theory will forgive my tendency to use these terms at times interchangeably. I do have a preference, however, for using terms like "social values" when referring to dominant social patterns or norms, and "ethics" when referring to ethical obligations in conjunction with some kind of moral imperative, as is the case when discussing ethical issues affecting the elderly. My ambivalence toward these terms reflects my own conviction that many of the ethical issues facing us might be changed or alleviated were we to espouse or adopt different or new social values. And, frankly, we are faced daily with conflicts, if not clashes, in our discussion of "ethics" and "values." For example, in his work *Social Work with the Aging*, Professor Louis Lowy (1979) defines social work as a "normative profession and values have a significant impact on its practice. Values are conceptions of preferred and admirable things or characteristics of people", and (as) "preferred stances of thinking, feeling and doing. They affect the people toward whom practice is directed, as well as the quality of social work."

For social workers in North America, "two values have dominated (their) practice: the worth, dignity and uniqueness of the individual and the right to self-determination by individuals, groups, or constituents in a community" (pp. 53-54).

From my earlier remarks it should be apparent that I do not see these two values of the social work profession as implicit or as "preferred" or "admirable" in our inherited Protestant work ethic.

I suggested earlier that for many individuals in our society our domination by mechanical time for most of our lives has left us weakened or depleted as human beings when we find ourselves later in life suddenly overwhelmed with time on our hands. I suggest that our situation is further exacerbated if the conclusions and warnings of cultural historians like Christopher Lasch (1978) have any validity. Last Christmas I gave a paperback copy of his controversial work, *The Culture of Narcissism: American Life in an Age of Diminishing Expectations,* to each of my three daughters with the inscription that this is an important book because it says a lot about the kind of world you are inheriting and will have to cope with and shape. I think it is also an important work for all of us today. Concerns similar to those of Lasch are contained in the late E.F. Schumacher's *Small is Beautiful* and also in a quite challenging if not disturbing work by Jeremy Rifkin and Ted Howard entitled, *The Emerging Order: God in the Age of Scarcity*.

Some of the warnings and conclusions contained in these works are particularly disturbing because they are being made at a time in our nation's history when, despite the usual concerns about inadequate funds and programs not only for the elderly, but for all disadvantaged minority groups, our standard of living and life expectancy are at an all-time high. Or is it that we are on the threshold of new social demands and conditions requiring new ways of coping and social planning? Or, as some commentators would have us believe, are we already over the hill and is it too late to meet the challenge constructively?

Lasch's work reminds me somewhat of Pope Innocent III's treatise entitled *On the Misery of the Human Condition*, which was an indictment of social conditions in the twelfth century. Lasch argues that a "crisis of confidence has gripped all capitalistic countries" and that the international dimensions of the current malaise cannot simply be attributed to a "failure of nerve."

> Bourgeois society seems everywhere to have used up its store of constructive ideas. It has lost both the capacity and the will to confront the difficulties that threaten to overwhelm it. The political crisis of capitalism reflects a general crisis of western culture, which reveals itself in a pervasive despair of understanding the course of modern history or of subjecting it to rational direction. Liberalism, the political theory of the ascendant bourgeoisie, long ago lost the capacity to explain events in the world of the welfare state and the multinational corporation; nothing has taken its place. Politically bankrupt, liberalism is intellectually bankrupt as well. The sciences it has fostered, once confident of their ability to dispel the darkness of the ages, no longer provide satisfactory explanations of the phenomena they profess to elucidate (p. xiii).

This, for Lasch, is how it viewed "from the top"—by those in positions of power—those who govern, control the media, and determine the directions that science and technology shall follow. Viewed from the bottom by the common man, the future is equally bleak. However, the general distrust of the bureaucratic power of those in decision-making positions may become the basis for a new power structure rooted in self-government, self-help, and local action and initiative. The unwillingness not only of the common man but of the managerial elite to participate in a political system wherein people see themselves as consumers of "prefabricated spectacles," may constitute the basis for a major political revolt.

Lasch's book is about an American way of life that is dying—"the culture of competitive individualism (and) the pursuit of happiness"—two marks of the "narcissistic preoccupation with the self" which also involves a devaluation, if not a denial, of any sense of future and therefore of past as well. Both *history* and *time* have lost their meaning for those engulfed by an overwhelming sense of *anxiety* .

Events have rendered liberationist critiques of modern society hopelessly out of date—and much of an earlier Marxist critique as well. Many radicals still direct their indignation against the authoritarian family, repressive sexual morality, literary censorship, the work ethic, and other foundations of bourgeois order that have been weakened or destroyed by advanced capitalism itself. These radicals do not see that the "authoritarian personality" no longer represents the prototype of the economic man. Economic man himself has given way to the psychological man of our times—the final product of bourgeois individualism. The new narcissist is haunted not by guilt but by anxiety.

The narcissist has no interest in the future because, in part, he has so little interest in the past. He finds it difficult to internalize happy associations or to create a a store of loving memories with which to face the latter part of his life, which under the best of conditions always brings sadness and pain. In a narcissistic society—a society that gives increasing prominence and encouragement to narcissistic traits—the cultural devaluation of the past reflects not only the poverty of the prevailing ideologies, which have lost their grip on reality and abandoned the attempt to master it, but the poverty of the narcissist's inner life (p. xvi).

For Lasch, the narcissistic preoccupation with the self whose end result is a state of chronic anxiety, is accompanied not only by a denial of past but embodies "the despair of a society that cannot face the future" (p. xviii).

Whereas Lasch speaks of "American Life in an Age of Diminishing Expectations," authors Jeremy Rifkin and Ted Howard (1979) in their work *The Emerging Order* speak of "God in the Age of Scarcity." They argue that American society has entered an age of scarcity, that the American dream of "unlimited wealth" is clearly a delusion, and that our nation has been plunged into a spiritual void. Rifkin and Howard founded and directed The Peoples Bicentennial Commission in 1971 and currently are co-directors of the Peoples Business Commission in Washington, D.C. Their approach is a theological one that many will find disturbing if not alarming. They focus on the vitality within the Charismatic and evangelical community which they view as providing the basis for a major spiritual revival which will in turn be transformed into a major social reawakening by the year 2000. They "believe that all of the major religious groupings will begin to reassess their own role in American life as the nation moves from the age of growth to the age of limits." What they envision is a second Protestant Reformation to replace the "symbiotic relationship" that they assert exists between the notion of an age of expansion and the sixteenth century Protestant Reformation. They contend that:

. . .we are nearing the end of an epoch that stretched across a half millennium of history. The age of expansion, with its faith in unlimited economic growth and the governing truths of science and technology, is about to give way to a new age of scarcity and economic contraction, an age so utterly different from our own that any serious attempt to give form and substance to it all but boggles the mind (pp. xiii-ix).

The basis for this new movement or reawakening rests on the spiritual energy vested in the millions of "Charismatics, whose belief in supernatural gifts of faith healing, speaking in tongues and prophesy represent a monumental assault on the modern age itself" (Ibid p. xi). At the center of their theological beliefs is a widely ac-

cepted redefinition in Genesis of the relationship between God and
his creatures.

> Its redefinition changes the entire relationship of human be-
> ings to both God and the temporal world. In the beginning,
> God says to Adam 'have dominion over the fish of the sea
> and over the birds of the air and over every living thing that
> moves upon the earth.' 'Dominion,' which (they argue)
> Christian theology has for so long used to justify people's
> unrestrained pillage and exploitation of the natural world,
> has suddenly and dramatically been reinterpreted. Now, ac-
> cording to (their) new definition of dominion, God's first in-
> struction to the human race is to serve as a steward and pro-
> tector over all his creation (p. 70).

What is impressive about this movement is that it originates
within the more conservative religious groups our nation—groups
which until recently were not viewed as having a positive interest in
social order and reform. A careful listening, however, to their
message suggests that what they propose by way of social reform goes
far beyond anything that we traditionally associate with liberation
theologies or with moderate or ultraliberal religious pronouncements.
Although the National Council of Churches, for example, has traditionally been identified with support or advocacy of ultraliberal, if
not, at times, leftist proposals for social reform, it was their Director
of the then Department of Religious Liberty, the Rev. Dean M.
Kelley, a Methodist, who in 1972 in a book entitled *Why Conservative
Churches Are Growing,* drew our attention to the amazing growth of
evangelical and Pentacostal churches and analyzed the decline in
membership in liberal and established churches.

One underlying theme throughout his work is that efforts by the
more liberal churches at ecumenism, dialogue among all religious
faiths, and social reform and church renewal have met with little success and that those involved in these efforts not only lack the
wherewithal to effect such changes, but their actions have tended to
thwart rather than encourage success. The growing attraction of
charismatic and evangelical churches and sects, according to Kelley,
lies in their ''strictness'' which ''is the consequence and evidence of
the seriousness of meaning'' (p. 174). They zero in on providing a

sense of purpose for life by giving their followers a sense of coherence and meaning rooted in a firm context of religious experience. Churches that are preoccupied with programs and movements and fail to address this human need are bound to fail in their appeal. The "exclusiveness" or "strictness" of conservative churches is a testimony to their commitment to what they consider the main function and purpose of true religion (p. 176). Implicit in their appeal is a rejection of the notion that the religion, in order to be effective and successful, must be restrained, rational, and receptive and responsive to outside criticism. For Kelley, it is precisely in their untamed fervor and appeal that their success lies.

It is intriguing that cultural historians like Lasch, using Freudian and post- or neo-Marxian critiques of the social order, should share not only the concerns of right wing religious groups about the crisis we are involved in, but some of their proposals as well.

In a section of his book entitled Narcissism and Old Age, Lasch states that "men have always feared death and longed to live forever." Prelates in the churches are no exception. In a recent *Newsweek* (March 17, 1980) review of Morgan's biography of W. Somerset Maugham, the reviewer pointed out that Maugham, along with Konrad Adenauer, Charles Lindbergh, and Pope Pius XII and others, had been patients of the Swiss physician, Paul Niehans, known for his rejuvenation therapy which involved injecting cells scraped from unborn sheep into the body. For Lasch, ". . .the fear of death takes on new intensity in a society that has deprived itself of religion and shows little interest in posterity." He argues that "our attitudes towards aging are not accidental," that they are products of long-term social changes that

. . .have redefined work, created a scarcity of jobs, devalued the wisdom of the ages, and brought all forms of authority (including the authority of experience) into disrepute (p. 209).

Because these attitudes are rooted in social causes, "merely propagandizing on their behalf or formulating more humane policies will not be enough to alleviate their lot. . .Nothing short of a complete reordering of work, education, the family—of every important institution—will make old age more bearable'' (p. 209). The plight of the elderly is especially critical in a narcissistic society because they have so little to fall back on or to look forward to, and are caught up in ''irrational panic'' and anxiety.

> This irrational terror of old age and death is closely associated with the emergence of the narcissistic personality as the dominant type of personality structure in contemporary society. Because the narcissist has so few inner resources, he looks to others to validate his sense of self. He needs to be admired for his beauty, charm, celebrity, or power—attributes that usually fade with time. Unable to achieve satisfying sublimations in the form of love and work, he finds that he has little to sustain him when youth passes him by. He takes no interest in the future and does nothing to provide himself with the traditional consolations of old age, the most important of which is the belief that future generations will in some sense carry on his life's work (p. 210).

In former times one of the great consolations of old age was that our accomplishments—the love and energy invested in our children and our work—would be passed on and remembered by our survivors, by future generations. The time dimension, namely future expectations and their personal rewards in the *now* of one's declining years, gave meaning and comfort because of each individual's involvement in past and future generations. Those with a sense of lived and anticipated future created a past worth remembering by them and their survivors and successors. The marks of a society without any sense of future are, for Lasch, easily recognized.

> The emergence of the narcissistic personality reflects among other things a drastic shift in our sense of historical time. Narcissism emerges as the typical form of character structure in a society that has lost interest in the future. Psychiatrists who tell parents not to live through their offspring; married couples who postpone or reject parenthood, often for good practical reasons; social reformers who urge zero population growth, all testify to a pervasive uneasiness about reproduction—to widespread doubts, indeed, about whether our

society should reproduce itself at all. Under these conditions, the thought of our eventual supersession and death becomes utterly insupportable and gives rise to attempts to abolish old age and to extend life indefinitely. When men find themselves incapable of taking an interest in earthly life after their own death, they wish for eternal youth, for the same reason they no longer care to reproduce themselves (p. 211).

My purpose in pursuing this approach to my subject was not to provide concrete solutions to the problems I've presented or raised. Nor would I dare to say that my approach is either the best or only one. What I did hope to achieve was to encourage those of you who have doubts about our ability to continue a business-as-usual social policy to read, discuss, and question the validity of points or problems raised in your own thinking. For those with no reservations about the course of American social policy and that prevalent in most in-dustralized Western societies, I hope to have at least sown some seeds of moral and intellectual curiosity, if not concern.

When Dr. John Knowles assumed the presidency of the Rockefeller Foundation in 1974 he invited four distinguished scholars to meet with him and focus their discussion on current cultural and ethical problems. One of the participants, Hannah Arendt, was quoted in the Foundation's *Values in Contemporary Society* (March 1974) as suggesting that it "would be a great mistake. . .to believe that (one foundation) can solve the basic problems of the era; no single one of us can do that." She then added, "But there is something else that one can do, . . .and that is to prepare an atmosphere in which things are being talked about (p. 10). Here then is one objective: to create a climate in which those of us concerned with problems of the elderly can meet, and in Buber's sense, enjoin one another in "dialogue." As a working paper for such dialogues I recommend to you the *Final Report for the American Values and the Elderly Project* (December 31, 1979) conducted by the University of Michigan-Wayne State University Institute of Gerontology. There is one project that the group is engaged in that may be of interest to our participants. They are preparing a handbook entitled *Values and Decision Making for the Elderly: A Handbook for Practitioners*. Their section on "Practitioner Decisions" interested me, because I found a similarity in our respective approaches—which I shall call a "life" or "situation ethic" approach. Implicit in this approach is the assumption that who finally makes decisions and what is finally decided may differ with each concrete situation.

In many ways the Institute's approach is similar to that of such proponents of situation ethics as Professor Joseph Fletcher, Bishop J.A.T. Robinson, and the late Martin Buber. Justice Oliver Wendell Holmes summed up this approach in his famous dictum that "General principles do not always decide concrete cases." Those of us who have followed the Golden Rule may also wish to consider in the light of this approach the validity of rewording it so that it reads, "Do unto others as they would have it done unto themselves." Or, as Buber (Hodes, 1972) said, "I have no rigid principles. There is what has to be done here and now. I have only a direction and my senses, and I act according to the situation" (pp. 218-219).

Before concluding, I feel compelled to provide something more than the possibility of providing a climate or ethos for further dialogue. My reading, my experience, and my concern about improving the quality of life for the elderly suggest that we focus our conversations and thoughts on the following themes and considerations:

First, as the title of my chapter suggests, that we examine critically the social values of American society, paying special attention to a review of the validity of traditional values like the Protestant work ethic, growth, success, technological achievement, and the youth-culture syndrome. What role can and should humanistic and spiritual values play in our thinking and planning? Is a sense of past and future necessary for humans of every age in a viable and healthy society?

Second, that we focus on the entire spectrum of the "aging process" and not simply on "the elderly," because as Dr. Bernice Neugarten (1979) points out in an article entitled, *Time, Age, and the Life Cycle*, it is no longer sufficient to say that "the child is father of the man." In her article, she develops the implications of a "new age-irrelevant society." Our approach must also be a multigenerational one that accepts as its premise the validity of the "fluid" life cycle, as well as the need for the interaction, and in some cases, the intervention of all age groups in dealing with one another's problems (pp. 887ff.).

Third, that we consider the role that volunteers and people who care can play in recovering and imparting a sense of the worth and dignity of every human being. In this regard, can professionalism function effectively without the caring component or relationship? In an article entitled *Some Ways for Dealing with the Negative Social Consequences of Technology,* Dr. Hans R. Huessy, (1979) Professor of Psychiatry at the University of Vermont, notes: "Providing. . .caring is a strenuous task. First, these caring relationships are not controlled by appointments or eight-hour shifts. Caring does not go off duty. . . . Caring requires constant interaction between the provider and the person for whom he is caring. So a caring relationship is the complement of a professional relationship. One of the hallmarks of professionalization is that it limits the interaction between professional and client. . . .The caring relationship differs (in this respect) from the professional relationship" (pp. 193-203).

Although mental health literature is filled with attempts to find professionalized ways of providing caring, Dr. Huessy is "convinced that this is a dream never to be realized. The professional role. . .is (1) to make the decision that a caring setting is needed; and (2) to see to it that the setting has stability over time. Caring cannot be institutionalized, but we can create institutions in which caring can occur" (p. 10).

I should like to add that it was Dr. Huessy's father, the late Professor Eugen Rosenstock-Huessy, Professor of Social Philosophy at Dartmouth College, who helped develop in me a sense of the importance of caring. In his work, *Out of Revolution: The Autobiography of Western Man* (1975), he defined the task for the postwar community, as that of the "survival of a more truly human society" (p. 740).

Finally, I would recommend to all of you that you take seriously the approach to the problems of our society of Maggie Kuhn and her Gray Panthers—which is certainly a multigenerational, age-irrelevant one filled with ample doses of caring. (See Chapter 4, Older Persons and the Democratic Process, Lydia Bragger).

REFERENCES

Butler, R.N., *Why survive: Being old in America.* New York: Harper & Row, 1975.

Hodes, A., *Encounter with Martin Buber.* London: Penguin Books, 1972.

Huessy, E.R., *Out of Revolution: The Autobiography of Western Man*. Norwich, Vermont: Argo Books, 1975.

Huessy, H.R., Some ways for dealing with the negative social consequences of technology. *Technology and Society*, 1979, *1*, pp. 193-203.

The Institute of Gerontology, The University of Michigan, *American values and the elderly*. December 31, 1979.

Jones, W.T., *Approaches to ethics*. New York: McGraw Hill, 1977.

Kelley, D.M., *Why conservative churches are growing*. New York: Harper & Row, 1962.

Lasch, C., *The culture of narcissism*. New York: W. W. Norton, 1978.

Lowy, L. *Social work with the aging*. New York: Harper & Row, 1979.

Mumford, L., *Technics and Civilization*. New York: Harcourt Brace & World, 1963.

Neugarten, B., Time, age, and the life cycle. *The American Journal of Psychiatry*, July, 1979, 136:7.

Rifkin, J., with Howard, T., *The emerging order*. New York: G.P. Putnam's Sons, 1979.

The Rockefeller Foundation, *Values in Contemporary Society*. March 1974.

Sombart, W., *The quintessence of capitalism*. New York: E.P. Dutton, 1915.

Van Tassel, D.D., (Ed.) *Aging, death, and the completion of being*. Philadelphia: University of Pennsylvania Press, 1979.

Williams, R.M. Jr., *American society*. New York: Alfred A. Knopf, 1970.

Chapter 3

HISTORICAL PERSPECTIVES ON THE ROLE OF THE ELDERLY
The Most Ancient Evidence

Gerald A. Larue

It should not be surprising to discover that present day fears and hopes, beliefs and questions echo those of our ancient ancestors. Some of the oldest surviving literature in our Western civilization derives from the ancient Near East and includes the cultures of Egypt, Sumer, Babylon, and Canaan.[1] These sources which involve myths, legends, historical accounts, folk concepts, law, and social customs, will be discussed under six headings: the concept of family and family tensions, the vulnerability of the aged, the attitude towards aging, the significance of life experiences, insights for our time, and some suggestions.

THE CONCEPT OF FAMILY AND FAMILY TENSIONS

As in modern times, the most importannt social unit was the family. The family included the father and one or more wives and concubines, their children, and perhaps slaves and children born to slave women impregnated by the father. Within the family, males were more important than females, the firstborn son more important

than subsequent sons, and children of concubines could be recognized as legitimate family heirs. Children born to slave women might be
recognized as heirs if, for example, the father publicly admitted they
were his sons.[2] In dire circumstances children might be sold into
slavery.

Marriages were generally arranged by the participant families
and the groom was expected to pay a marriage price to the father of
the bride to compensate for the loss of children who would be
recognized as progeny of the groom's family. Within the family structure, the father was the dominant and most powerful figure; the
mother had lesser stature and exercised authority by more subtle
means than the father.

Because the structure of marriage and the family differed so
much from that of our society, it may be important to note that feelings of love, bonding, affection, joy in sharing are all manifested in
the literature of the ancient Near East. Today, in many parts of the
Muslim world arranged marriages are common, males are dominant,
and it is possible to have more than one wife. Many of us have
witnessed the tender affection, deep loyalty, warm love and caring expressed in these families. Moreover, the power of the wife, though
limited by status, is not to be underestimated.

One other pattern operated almost universally: the concept of
familial unity and the consequent defective sense of individualism.
An individual had significance primarily as a member of a larger
unit: a family, a clan, a tribe, a city, or a class within the city. Such
membership placed unique responsibilities upon group members.
Harm to one was harm to all, injury to one member called for retalia-
tion and an equal injury to a member of the other group. When this
idea passed into law it took the form of the *lex talionis,* the law of exchange, which called for an eye for an eye and a tooth for a tooth from
the offender. In more sophisticated law, physical retribution was
replaced by a fine.[3] Thus what one individual did affected the health
and welfare of the total group. There was a generally accepted code of
social behavior and the pressure to conform to that code was expressed
throughout all levels of society. For example, should a son prove to be
a misfit, a nonconformist, incompetent, or a troublemaker, his
behavior reflected on the entire family unit and all were embarrassed.
Parents were advised to discipline their sons and should a son prove

to be unmanageable or incorrigible, he was to be disowned and discarded.

Age in itself carried weight in families. The older brother was the person in charge, the man of authority. In the fascinating Egyptian *Tale of the Two Brothers,* (which may be the source of the idea for the Joseph and Potiphar account in the Bible) two brothers lived together. The older, named Anubis, was married and was in charge of the house, the fields, and the animals. The younger brother, Bata, worked with and for his brother. When Anubis' wife attempted to seduce Bata and was rejected, she pretended to have been manhandled by him. Anubis, infuriated at this supposed humiliation of his wife, attempted to kill Bata. Bata fled and was saved by a lake filled with crocodiles magically interposed between the two men by the sun god. Across this lake he shouted the true story of the attempted seduction, and to verify his interpretation hacked off his penis and cast it into the lake. Anubis, returned home and killed his wife; Bata sought his fortune elsewhere. Throughout the story, although Bata is the hero, the power and the authority are vested in Anubis as the elder brother.

Sons often followed in their father's footsteps and were expected to inherit the father's job or role. Thus the father assumed the role of educator. Much of the ancient wisdom attributed to elders has come to us in the form of collections of proverbs, maxims, and aphorisms in collections attributed to pharaohs, viziers, and leaders or teachers in the schools of the wise, which were generally court-supported institutions for training young men for government sayings. The advice is much the same whether the precepts were taught in Eygpt or Mesopotamia: establish a family, conform to social norms, express quiet compliance with the established order, avoid quarrels and do not become involved in the altercations of others, do not cheat or steal, honor your parents, and in general be a solid, supportive citizen.

Ptah-hotep, the famous vizier to the Egyptian court of King Izezi during the fifth dynasty (25th century B.C.) made this comment on aging:

Old age has arrived, elderliness is here, feebleness has come, dotage is at hand. The heart (mind) responds drowsily each day, eyes are weak, ears deaf, strength dissipates through weariness. The mouth is silent and cannot speak; the heart (mind) is forgetful and cannot recall yesterday. Bones ache all over, good has become evil. The nose is stuffed up and cannot breathe and taste is gone. What old age does to men is evil in every respect.[4]

In this mood the vizier asks that his son be allowed to take his place. In anticipation of acceptance of his request, he provided his son with a collection of sayings that represented his accumulated wisdom and which are designed to guide the young man in the traditional office.

There seems to have been no given term of office and no age of compulsory retirement. It does not take much imagination to envision young men waiting with differing degrees of impatience for the opportunity to occupy posts held by their elders, despite the fact that the old men might be their fathers or close relatives. One ancient tale, the story of Ahikar, reflects this impatience.[5]

Ahikar was grand vizier to Sennacherib, king of Assyria, during the seventh century B.C. Ahikar was wealthy, powerful, and wise but had no son to succeed him. Because of the importuning of his sister, he adopted his nephew Nadan and began to train the boy for the post of court vizier. The young man was deluged with proverbial lore to provide a saying or maxim for guidance in any situation. But Nadan grew impatient and felt he had learned enough. When he overheard the king say that so long as Ahikar lived the old man's power and wealth were untouchable, he decided to take action. He convinced himself that Ahikar "is grown old and stands at the door of the grave and his intelligence is gone and his understanding diminished.[6] By forging treasonable documents, Nadan betrayed Ahikar and the aged vizier was condemned to death. Through a plot he was saved from execution and a condemned criminal died in his stead—all of this without the knowledge of Nadan or the monarch. Nadan became vizier. His abilities were soon tested and a threat from the Egyptians revealed his lack of training. At this point, King Sennacherib expressed the wish that Ahikar was still around, and, of course, was told that the old vizier was indeed still alive. Ahikar was restored to office, solved the problem with Egypt and punished the ungrateful nephew by chaining him, beating and starving him, and what may have been worse, subjecting him to an unending barrage of aphorisms and parables associated with ingratitude until Nadan died.

Tensions between youth and age are also echoed in the central Babylonian creation myth where young gods defeat the older gods.[7] The goddess Tiamat (salt water) and the god Apsu (fresh water), the parents of creation, produced offspring who in turn produced grand-children that drove the old gods mad with their incessant noise. Apsu decided to eliminate the noise by killing the offspring. When the young gods learned of this plan they rebelled and Apsu was killed. Tiamat, furious over the death of her mate, created horrendous monsters to eliminate the younger gods. Led by Marduk, the supreme god of Babylon, the young gods defeated the monsters, killed the mother goddess, split her body in two and used one half to form the arch of the heavens and the other the foundation of the earth.

Fear of the young by the aged appears in the Canaanite myth of Ba'al.[8] Ba'al, the god of fertilizing rain, contested and overcame his brother Yam, the sea and river god, for control of the earth. To sym-bolize his new authority Ba'al needed a castle. With his sister Anat he approached the mother goddess Asherah to ask her to intercede with the father god, El. Their approach terrified Asherah. Later, when Anat confronted El, she bullied him, despite his status as god the father, threatening to bash in his head if he did not accede to her wishes. He was properly obedient to the demands of his violent daughter.

The tension between young and old in the ancient Near Eastern literature seems to reflect the fact that the elderly are in positions of power and control and the young must approach them for basic needs or wait for the old to die before assuming important offices.

It is not suprising to discover that the wise elders developed laws for protection of parents. These laws were divine laws and were always issued under the imprimatur of one god or another. They were to be obeyed and carried through, not ignored or questioned.

In the first half of the nineteenth century B.C., Lipit-Ishtar, ruler of the Sumerians, produced a code under the aegis of Anu the sky god and Enlil the wind god. In the prologue he announced that he had developed, through law, familial solidarity:

I made the father support his children and I made the children support the father; I made the father stand by his children; I made the children stand by their father. . . .[9]

During the late eighteenth century, B.C. when Hammurabi became king of Babylon, his law code, sanctioned by the sun god Shamash, made it clear that the father was in complete control.[10] Should a son strike his father, his hand was chopped off (195). The father could adopt or disinherit children, sell his daughters into slavery, and control the destiny of his offspring. Middle Assyrian laws which were developed during the fifteenth and twelfth centuries B.C. placed the father in full control of property.[11] At his death, when the property was divided, the oldest son received a major portion.

THE VULNERABILITY OF THE AGED

Aging may be accompanied by physical and mental deterioration, and when persons in power show signs of weakening they become vulnerable. In the ancient world, vitality of mind and body were essentials of leadership.

In Egypt, despite the belief in the pharaoh as an incarnate deity, it was important that the ruler demonstrate physical prowess. Some scholars suggest that at one time the pharaoh reigned for a given time (30 years has been an estimate) before being put to death and replaced. By the first dynasty (c. 3100 B.C.) this practice had been abandoned and was replaced by a Sed festival symbolizing the renewal of the monarchy. Part of the ritual involved a run of four ritual courses by the pharaoh who wore only a kilt and the crown of Upper Egypt and carried the royal scepter and flail. The rite was a rejuvenation ceremony, renewing and strengthening the king's life and representing the regeneration of his vigor as the dynamic center of the empire. Symbolically, at least, the Sed festival rendered the pharaoh safe from the ravages of old age.

But elderliness could imply vulnerability, and one Egyptian myth tells of a plot by humans to overthrow Ra, the aged sun god who had created them and with whom they lived:

> Now his Majesty had become old. His bones were silver, his flesh was gold and his hair genuine lapis lazuli.[12]

When Ra became aware of the plot, he withdrew, together with the other gods, from the world of humans to live in heaven. He plotted to destroy his creation, not by flood as in Mesopotamian myths, but by the sword of the lioness-headed goddess Sekhmet (Hathor). Sekhmet set about her appointed task, but darkness fell before she completed her work. During the night, the gods relented and sought ways to forestall the slaughter of mankind. They manufactured red beer and poured it in great pools on the earth. The next morning, as Sekhmet descended to continue her work, she saw her reflection in the red beer which she assumed were pools of blood. She paused, tasted the liquid, and continued to imbibe until she became drunk and abandoned her mission. Thus humans were saved by beer—a deliverance that was faithfully re-enacted with joy in the temples of the goddess.

But the aged Ra was a potential victim not only of humans but also of his fellow gods. Divine beings had many names, but to know the secret name, the hidden name, was to have power over the god; hence such names were not commonly revealed.[13] The goddess Isis wanted to know Ra's secret name and she plotted to acquire it:

> The Divine One had become old. His mouth quivered and he dribbled spit on the ground.[14]

Isis kneaded the spit with clay and fashioned a serpent which bit Ra and poisoned him. Because no one knew the nature of the poison, all known remedies were useless and the aged god writhed in helpless agony. Isis was called, but before she healed Ra she extracted from him his secret name.

ATTITUDES TOWARDS AGING

There was a time, according to the Sumerian king list, when people lived incredibly long lives. The text begins:

> When kingship was first lowered from heaven, kingship began in (the city of) Eridu. In Eridu, Alulium was king and reigned for 28,800 years. Alalgar ruled 36,000 years. Two kings ruled there for 64,8000 years.[15]

The text next moves to the city of Bad-tibara where En-men-lu-Anna ruled for 43,200 years, En-men-gal-Anna for 28,800 years and the god-shepherd Dumuzi reigned for 36,000 years.

The list continues up to the time of the flood. Following the flood the kings ruled for shorter periods: for example Kalibum ruled 960 years, Qalumum for 840 years, Zuqaqip for 900 years, and so on. The closer one came to the time of the composition of the list (end of the third millennium B.C.) the shorter the reigns became. Hence in the city of Ur, Mes-Anna-pada ruled 80 years, Mes-kiag-Nanna reigned 25 years, Balulu 36 years.

Why these tremendous records in longevity? Did the ancients possess some secret formula to prolong life? Most will recognize a patter familiar from the book of Genesis in the Bible where pre-flood heroes lived for hundreds of years. What appears to lie behind these reports is the awareness that humans have lived on earth for a very long time and that at that time there was no known human history to bridge the gap between the time when the gods created the world and made humans their servants, the flood when they became disaffected with their creation and attempted to destroy it, and the post-flood period when human history began again. To cover these long gaps in time concerning which almost nothing was known, ancient writers constructed the king list of known hero-kings, but gave each an incredibly long reign. It should be noted that almost nothing is said about what took place during the kings' reign; they simply occupied the throne for thousands or hundreds of years.

As the list draws closer to the time when human memory, human records, and folklore can place restrictions on reigns, the time is shortened to normal periods. In other words, there is absolutely no evidence that in ancient times monarchs ruled for hundreds or thousands of years. In fact, in view of poor sanitation, it is certain that many humans died in childhood and that life was even shorter than it is today.

Although old age was not to be desired, it was, for the most part, accepted as a reality one could not alter. Some Egyptian doctors produced mixtures that were supposed to eliminate the signs of aging.[16] For example, to prevent gray hair one took blood from the neck of the gabgu bird and mingled it with balsam and rubbed it in the scalp. Another treatment called for the horn of a fawn, warmed in oil and rubbed on the scalp. Again, one might use the bile of many crabs or dried tadpoles crushed and mingled with oil. A more elaborate preparation required the womb of a cat warmed in oil mixed with the egg of the gabgu bird. Still another recipe included the roasted hoof of an ass, a dog's vulva, a black tapeworm and a worm found in dung, all of which was to be mixed with oil and gum and rubbed in the scalp.

Wrinkles were treated with incense cake mixed with wax, fresh olive oil, Cyperus and fresh milk and used for 6 days. Egyptian attempts to erase the signs of aging were probably no more effective that those used today.

The Mesopotamians were perhaps a bit more realistic. They wished the aging process could be halted or reversed, but they knew the wish was futile. The story of Gilgamesh dramatized the issue.[17] Gilgamesh is listed in the Sumerian king list as the fifth king in the first dynasty of the city of Uruk, which would suggest that he reigned about the middle of the third millennium. The legends that developed about him record his desperate attempt to acquire some sort of immortality. At first he sought to achieve lasting fame through his unbridled energy which resulted in the exploitation of the citizenry and the offending of their sensibilities. He sought fame through heroic deeds, but in this venture he offended the gods, and his dearest friend died a lingering death in Gilgamesh's arms. Terrified by this death and now keenly aware of his own mortality, he sought a way to extend life. He journeyed to the underworld and visited Utnapishtim, an ancient kinsman who, together with his wife, had been granted immortality by the gods. Utnapishtim, however, had earned his gift when the gods attempted to destroy humankind by flood and Utnapishtim had constructed a monstrous boat, took pairs of all animals with him, and had thus saved the life of the world. His immortality was a reward, and the event could not be repeated for Gilgamesh.

Almost as a consolation, Utnapishtim told Gilgamesh of a magic plant which grew at the bottom of the sea—a plant called "the old man becomes young," and which had powers of rejuvenation. Gilgamesh acquired the plant, but decided to save it until he was older. During his return to the world, he disrobed to bathe in a pool, carefully placing the plant aside. During his ablutions, a snake devoured the plant. This story explains why the snake sheds his skin, thereby renewing itself, while humans, alas, must continue to grow old and die.

Embedded within the story are some wonderful responses to life and living which are not out of touch with our modern setting. For example, as Gilgamesh began his journey to the underworld, he paused

at an inn where a barmaid attempted to dissuade him from his
fruitless search:

> Gilgamesh, where are you running?
> You won't find the immortal life you seek.
> When the gods created men
> They ordained death for men
> But kept immortality for themselves.
> So make merry night and day,
> Make every day a day of joy.
> Dance, play, day and night.
> Wear exciting garments
> Perfume your head. Refresh yourself with water.
> Cherish the child who takes your hand.
> Let your wife rejoice in your bosom.
> For this is the fate of man.

The story represents a way of dealing with life. It is a wise man's account of a pilgrimage, a fruitless search for the elixir of life, which led
the hero back to the starting point—his own city and his responsibilities as the king. It teaches that no one can defeat the divinely or-
dained fate of mankind, and that the best way to cope with mortality
is to fulfill one's own destiny to the utmost. Gilgamesh, the wise king
passed his story on, and as a wise man instructed his people out of his
experience.

The sobriquet "the old man who renews his youth" was used in
Egypt with reference to the sun god. Each morning the sun was born
anew a Khephre, the scarab beetle who rolled the ball of the sun into
the heavens. At noon, the sun was Ra, the vigorous one at the peak of
power. In the evening, the sun became Atum, the old man descending to the underworld. Each night the sun made the journey through
the hours of darkness to be reborn again as Khephre. No such rebirth
was promised to humans in this life; only in the world beyond death
could one be assured of overcoming mortality.

Advice, much like that given to Gilgamesh by the barmaid, was
available to the Egyptians. At banquets a blind harpist sang dirges
lamenting the brevity of life:

> O beneficent Prince, it is decreed
> And what is ordained by the decree is good,

That the bodies of men shall pass away and disappear
And that others shall come to succeed them.
I have heard the wisdom of (the vizier) Imhotep and (Prince)
    Hor Dadef
Which, because they wrote them are greatly treasured.
But consider what has happened to their tombs:
The walls have crumbled,
Their locations have disappeared
Just as if they had never been.
And think of this: no one returns from where they are
To describe their condition,
To tell us of their surroundings,
Or to comfort our hearts,
Or to guide us to the place where they have gone.
So anoint your heads with perfumed oils,
Dress in exquisite garments,
Scent your body with precious perfumes
Which are the gifts of the gods,
Occupy yourself with pleasure day by day,
And don't stop seeking enjoyment for yourself.
Man is not permitted to take his goods with him
And there has never been a man who once departed
Was able to return to earth.
Follow your heart's desire,
Seek personal happiness,
Order your earthly affairs so that
They may minister to your heart's desire,
For ultimately the day of mourning comes,
When the dead will not hear the lamentations,
And the cries of grief will never make
The heart of he who is in the grave beat again.
So comfort yourself, forget these things
The best thing for you to do is to
Seek to fulfill your heart's desire so long as you live.[18]

INSIGHTS FOR OUR TIME

Perhaps what emerges immediately from this brief survey of
most ancient concepts is the striking alteration in the structure of the

family. Only in certain parts of the Arab world and perhaps in some ultraconservative Jewish and Christian households are there reminiscences of ancient patterns. We have moved from a corporate family structure to an emphasis upon individualism with the consequent loss of parental control. Many young people are still supported through high school and college, but by the age of eighteen many youths move out of the home and begin to establish separate identities. The change in the status of women also marks dramatic shifts in familial patterns. Women may acquire individual idenitities. Some marry and retain their maiden names; a few, having gone through divorce, have chosen to abandon both family and marriage names and have selected completely new names for themselves. Still others join their names with their husbands', and use both family names in hyphenated form.

Modern mobility can create great distances between family members, reducing immediate contact and diminishing the sense of responsibility. Parents rapidly lose control of their offspring, and as they age are left more and more to their own resources. Support for aging parents that once came through family channels now comes from the state.

The vulnerability of the aged remains. We are experiencing some impatience among rising young executives with elders who continue to hold office beyond the usual retirement age. It is not unreasonable to expect older persons to continue at jobs as long as they can because retirement funds are often inadequate. Some tension develops between the young who are trained in new patterns, such as the use of computers, and who have little respect for time-tested methods of their elders. They suggest that older workers either keep up or drop out.

There is also growing evidence of verbal and physical expressions of anger against the weakness of aging persons. Some nursing home personnel become insensitive to senile and incontinent patients and express verbal and physical hostility. Even when the elderly person remains with the family, the best of intentions and the most sincere expression of love and caring can become tinged with impatience. In those situations where tolerance is limited, physical and mental abuse of the aged is not uncommon. It is clear from recent studies that abuse of the elderly is widespread.[19]

There are changing emphases in our belief systems with more

importance being given to the individual. Persons engage in individual meditation to get themselves right. There is greater stress on the oppositional potential of religion than ever before with anti-homosexuality, anti-abortion, anti-Equal Rights Amendment, anti-drug, and anti-liquor militancy. There is diminished emphasis on familial responsibilities and family bonding and concern. There is less emphasis on the afterlife and less emphasis upon judgment for behavior. This means that some behavioral controls emphasized in religious belief systems have been redirected and one can be deeply religious by being opposed to certain social practices and positions and by being concentrated upon one's self, but oblivious to familial responsibilities, including concern for the aged.

SOME SUGGESTIONS

1.   There is a growing need for educational emphasis on the total maturation process as inevitable in nature, and less emphasis upon the age differences that separate us into opposing groups. Such an emphasis calls for an awakening to the potential wonder and beauty in each phase of maturation; that is, the amazing possibilities in youth as well as in old age, and the recognition of the splendor of each and every year of human existence.

2.   There is need for awareness of the vulnerability of the aged. Many articles warn against financial abuse of older people by unscrupulous individuals but abuse stemming from anger and from love-hate relationships is only beginning to surface. Group discussion with older persons and with families caring for the elderly have brought to the surface impatience, anger, even hostility of children and grandchildren in familial settings, and of professionals in nursing homes and institutes for the aged. Because these feelings lie deep in the psyche and often emerge tinged with guilt which adds to the frustration, there is need for psychiatrists to participate in and contribute to our understanding of these feelings.

3.   Studies have been under way for some time dealing with the pathology of aging, with its despair, futility, and loneliness. Too many programs for the aged contribute to that emptiness of so many lives through "Let's do. . ." activities and the "Why don't cha. . ." advice. Far too many activities for the aging are not tied into life purposes, and activity for the sake of activity pales quickly.

More involvement with professional family counselors and psychiatrists is needed to help us develop programs and attitudes that have meaning as well as action.

4. The slowly developing interest in family history needs augmenting. Some families, using tape recorders, have begun "talking histories" and have encouraged older family members to recall childhood, romance, marriage, raising families, changing jobs, and confrontation with some of the most dramatic social and industrial changes the world has ever witnessed. The interest is not merely in the older generation as such, but also in an attempt of some youths to answer the "who am I?" question. This query requires more data than data of birth and social security number and seeks to discover a heritage. We need to educate our young people to listen and our elderly to share.

5. Finally, if we are to slow the disintegration of the family and the sense of uselessness that haunts so many of the elderly, we need an education in life, living, maturation, and death that begins at a very early age. What are the elements that make existence rich and warm, significant and meaning-filled? What are the life-patterns that strengthen human bonds, that diminish the toxic and expand the nourishing aspects of communication between persons? How do we live so that we achieve closure of relationships so that the torturous gaps and chasms that open and separate us and breed feelings of isolation and guilt are annealed or avoided? If such patterns exist, and they surely do, how do we discover them, share them and make them significant? We learn from our ancient past that elements for successful maturation or for troubled aging have been with us for a long time. Perhaps, now, we can extract the life-elevating components and transmit them.

REFERENCE NOTES

1. Biblical concepts have been discussed in G.A. Larue, Biblical mythology and aging. In *Gerontology in Higher Education*. Wadsworth, 1979, pp. 81ff.
2. Cf., for example, the law code of Hammurabi, Law #170.
3. Sumerian laws, for example, had less harsh penalties than Semitic law.

4. For a complete translation see J. Wilson, The instruction of the Vizier Ptah-Hotep. In J.B. Pritchard, *Ancient Near Eastern Texts Relating to the Old Testament* (Henceforth *ANET)* Princeton, 1950, pp. 412ff.

5. See the translation by Harris, Lewis, and Conybeare in R.H. Charles, (Ed.), (Vol. II), *The Apocrypha and Pseudepigrapha of The Old Testament.* Oxford, 1913, pp. 715ff.

6. Syriac version, 3:1, p. 740.

7. The Babylonian creation epic. cf. *ANET,* pp. 60ff.

8. Cf. Poems about Ba'al and Anath, *ANET,* pp. 129ff.

9. Cf. "Lipit-Ishtar code, prologue," *ANET,* p. 159

10. Cf. *ANET,* pp. 163ff.

11. Cf. The Middle Assyrian laws, *ANET,* pp. 180ff.

12. Cf. The book of the divine cow. In A. Piankoff, *The Shrines of Tut-ankh-Amon.* Bollingen Foundation, 1955, p. 27.

13. Note the significance of the revelation of the divine name "YHWH" in Exodus 3:13-16, and Exodus 6:3.

14. Cf. Erman, A. *Life in Ancient Egypt.*

15. Cf. The Sumerian King List. *ANET,* pp. 265ff.

16. Cf. The Papyrus Ebers.

17. Cf. The epic of Gilgamesh. *ANET,* pp. 72ff.

18. Cf. Erman, A. *The Ancient Egyptians.* Harper & Row, 1966, p. 183.

19. See, for example, *Elder Abuse in Massachusetts.* Published by the Legal Research and Services for the Elderly, June 1, 1979.

Chapter 4

OLDER PERSONS AND THE DEMOCRATIC PROCESS

Lydia Bragger

The democratic process unfortunately excludes many older individuals. Decisions for their lives are often made by others, and the elderly are made to feel powerless. How older persons live is largely determined by the values and attitudes of a society which devalues the elderly. Such a demeaning attitude is reflected in every area of older persons' lives. It is such treatment which gave rise to the Gray Panthers.

The Gray Panthers are young, middle-aged, and older activists and advocates for basic social change. Our goal is human liberation, particularly from the oppressive forces of agism, which seeks to alienate, segregate, and regulate whole generations of people on the basis of age. We are not a homogenous mass and we feel that if we are going to have a part in planning our own destiny, we will have to stand up and be counted and educate society as to what old people are like today.

Racism and sexism have been with us for a long while. Now, within the last few years, we have become of a new ism—agism—which is destructive to all ages. As chairperson of the National Gray Panthers Media Watch, I am particularly concerned about the media and the way it perpetuates and encourages agism by the negative portrayal of older persons.

First, however, I should like to discuss older people today and the democratic process, and some of the reasons that we do not feel that we have much influence on the decisions that determine how we live.

Society forces older persons into boxes (as it does with all age groups) and we are oppressed by many factors; for example, forced retirement, a waste of human resources, fixed income, and loss of social status (unless you are rich). A whole gamut of pressures is directed from a society convinced that life is over at sixty-five. Society still accepts the out-of-date myths about old people, and pushes the old aside, out of the way, out of sight if possible, so as not to be reminded of the horrible future generally accepted for old age. Housing is one indication of the worth and regard in which the old are held. New York has its SRO's, single-room occupancies, where the old are herded together with drug addicts, prostitutes, and mental patients.

In San Diego, a housing complex for the elderly has terraces facing a mortuary. Many cities have built apartment housing for the elderly in isolated areas that make it difficult, for many nearly impossible, to shop for even the necessities. In most senior centers, the old are paternalized, making them powerless. The list is long and tragic.

The stresses affecting the elderly are not unique, but they are multiple and pervasive. The elderly are faced with social role changes, mandatory retirement, bereavement, isolation, fears of crime and physical disability, and economic worries. The elderly account for 25 percent of all suicides, although they constitute 11 percent of the population.

The generation of the old is really a pioneer group. It is exciting to be old today: a challenge. We have better health, better education, and are more aware, as everyone is in this electronic age. Consequently, we feel that we have a greater responsibility to society, and we want to have the opportunity to carry out that responsibility and to make the contributions of which we are capable.

Every day 4000 Americans celebrate their sixty-fifth birthday by virtue of this chronological passage. Society arbitrarily labels them elderly, or with less polite euphemisms. Currently there are more than 23 million people over sixty-five years of age in this country, representing 11 percent of the population. The ranks of the over sixty-five have a net increase of 1,000 people. By the year 2000 it is predicted that there will be 30 million people over sixty-five in the United States, nearly 15 percent of the population. Those who reach the age of sixty-five are our survivors. A sixty-five year-old man now has a life expectancy of 13 years. At seventy-five he has another 9 years. A sixty-five year old woman has a life expectancy of 17 years. At seventy-five she has another 12 years. They have in one way or another survived the stress of this complex society. People are living longer, and it is exciting to learn that much of what was long considered aging is now diagnosed as disease, and that many of the ailments of the old can be treated.

Agism pervades our society, and it affects the old in every area of life. Disregarding our expectations, 75 percent of the elderly are fit and live at home; the remaining 25 percent include 5 percent in nursing homes and 20 percent community-based with ongoing multiple health impairments which put them at a high risk for future institutional care. The elderly, 11 percent of the total population, use one-third of the hospital beds, one-fourth of all medication prescribed, and 30 percent of the total health dollars spent. The majority of the old cannot afford proper medical care. Most are on fixed incomes. Doctors' fees are too high for many older people and consequently many become critically ill before medical care is sought. Preventive care becomes a luxury. This is another area where the old feel helpless and unable to bring about change.

Many doctors and health personnel are not trained to deal with their unique problems. Their medical conditions have not been considered interesting to teaching institutions, and the old are stereotyped as bothersome, cantankerous, and complaining patients. Much prejudice exists. The old are submitted to enormous emotional stresses and a low social position. Because of their need for medical services and their costlier illnesses, older patients require more physician time, more frequent hospital long-term care facilities, and more health agencies. Medicare, ironically, does not cover the afflictions that the old suffer from the most: loss of hearing—hearing aids are very costly; sight impairment—glasses today are very expensive; and dental care and dentures cost more than many old can afford.

In order to effectively meet the needs of the older people for high quality medical treatment, accurate diagnosis, and sensitive care, it is imperative that the special perspective of the particular body of knowledge known as "geriatric medicine" be introduced into the curricula of 114 medical schools (with approximately 40,000 medical students), into our intern and resident training, into our programs of continuing education, into schools of nursing, social work, and in training paraprofessionals and other health professionals. We know that working in this country today we have some 375,000 practicing physicians, many of whom are not equipped to meet the needs of to-day's 23 million old people, a situation which is likely to grow worse as the number of older people increases by almost 50 percent in the next 3 decades.

Many of the old have been brainwashed into believing the myths that are so prevalent about old age. This has made it impossible for them to be convinced that they can still function as normal human be-ings in their old age. These myths burden us:

> Old age is a diseased state.
> Old age is a mindless state.
> Old age is a sexless state.
> Old age is a useless state.
> Old age is a powerless state.
> Old age is a homogeneous state.
> Old age is a tranquil state.

We, the Gray Panther Media Watch, started monitoring the media nearly 4 years ago, because we believe that these myths are perpetuated to a large extent by the media, radio, television, and the press. However, television is the most pervasive medium. Ninety-seven percent of all homes have TV sets. Americans, mainly the very young, the old, and the poor, tune in about 6 hours a day—that's 2,400 hours a year. Between the ages of two to sixty-five, the average person will watch 9 full years of television.

These myths have subtly influenced us to write off our elders. Physicians have been cavalier in their treatment of the elderly; social services have been designed to tolerate the elderly, the work world has been impatient to move the elderly on. And, as we have become the elderly, some of us have docilely accepted these myths and have cooperated to become what these myths designated as our inevitable state.

> Even when their physical and mental health is excellent, men and women in the fifties, sixties, and seventies, sometimes exhibit an old-man and old-woman act as though they were tottering invalids on their last legs. Having a rigid, stereotyped, desexualized image of what an older person should be, they play the role with stubborn determination. The 'old person act' allows them to avoid responsibility toward themselves and others, and to evoke sympathy. It is a symptom of demoralization and giving up. (Butler & Lewis, 1976.)

Because of these myths, simple pains and aches become traumas. If we forget, it's because we are getting old and senile. Men over fifty become impotent. Women tend to believe all of the myths about sex after menopause, and become depressed. The myth of a sexless old age has made it nearly impossible for old people to be treated with respect and dignity in regard to their sexuality. The perpetuation of these myths has been destructive, and has created a sense of worthlessness in old people, making them feel that they have no contributions to make to society. The feeling of powerlessness is destructive and pervasive, and is caused, to a large extent, by a society that still regards us as what Maggie Kuhn, National Convenor of the Gray Panthers, calls "wrinkled babies." We are treated like children, paternalized. The image of the old, projected especially in the media, generalizes and portrays old people as decrepit, senseless, toothless, tasteless, sexless, as idiots, and on and on—everything negative.

The Gray Panthers Media Watch, through monitoring, complaining, and speaking out against this atrocious pattern of sterotyping, has seen positive changes take place in the media. There is a growing awareness that old people are indeed human beings with skills, experience, knowledge, and potential; and that life is a continuum and doesn't end at sixty-five. We see this new awareness revealed in more positive images of the older person shown in the media.

It is encouraging that more and more we are asked to speak about the problems and the joys of aging. We have seen a shift from curiosity about the old to genuine interest. There is an International Senior Citizen Association chaired at this time by a Gray Panther and a world assembly on aging was held in 1982. In television programming we now see more older people shown. Commercials are including old persons in the fun activities. There is a new magazine for the forty-five to sixty-five readership, *Prime Time*. There is a whole new yoga program for older persons. Intergenerational seminars are being held across the country. An article in the January 1980 issue of *Marketing Communications*, a trade magazine, entitled *The Mature Market Comes of Age*, explores the economic status of the older person.

In the near future, we, the old, expect to have much more involvement in the democratic process. We are going to make it happen. Opportunities to stay within the mainstream of society and to participate actively in helping solve this nation's problems are what the older people strongly desire and would welcome.

REFERENCES

Astor, D. *The mature market comes of age*. New York: *Marketing Communications*, January 1980, p. 40.

Butler, R.N., & Lewis, M.I. *Sex after sixty*. New York: Harper & Row, 1976.

Kuhn, M. *Maggie Kuhn on aging*. Philadelphia: Westminister Press, 1977.

National Council on Aging. Louis Harris & Associates, Public Opinion Study, 1975.

President's Commission on Mental Health, Sub-Panel on the Elderly. Fall 1977, p. 1.

President's Commission on Mental Health, Sub-Panel on the Elderly. Fall 1977, p. 2.

President's Commission on Mental Health, Sub-Panel on the Elderly. Fall 1977, p. 7.

Chapter 5

LEGAL PERSPECTIVES
Issues of Competency

George J. Alexander

The law of guardianship turns on a number of complex concepts. The three most important are: the concept of responsibility, notions of medical (especially psychiatric-psychological) and legal competence, and notions as to what constitutes basic procedural fairness. The legal perspective of each has changed appreciably over time and can be expected to continue to change. Some of the confusion concerning guardianship can be attributed to the tension among the ideas. Much more has to do with lethargy and some has to do with stupidity. I will refer throughout to something which I will call guardianship.

There is, of course, no single entity known as guardianship. Each state and the federal government have their own forms of guardianship. Some states have more than one form, such as, for example, California which has both conservatorship and guardianship. The procedures differ, as well as the names. The consequences of "guardianship" also differ. In many states they include the possibility of long-term institutionalization. In California, on the other hand, no psychiatric hospitalization is permitted unless a proceeding is separately brought for that purpose.

For the remainder of this discussion, however, I will refer to guardianship as though it were a unitary concept uniformly applied.

From such a standpoint, the following discussion does not require a greater level of detail.

I. The Recent Past

The major contribution of the recent past is its fundamental simplicity. Admittedly, the simplicity is somewhat enhanced by the level of generalization I have allowed myself. Nonetheless, there was a good conjunction of the three aforementioned considerations. The law tended to consider responsibility in polar terms. One was either sane and responsible, or insane and irresponsible.

The conclusion one drew led to a number of consequences that simultaneously required and justified surrogate property management and involuntary institutionalization. Little consideration appears to have been given to gradations. If one was not "responsible," it didn't matter whether one was old and senile, or young and bizarre. Neither psychiatric nor legal professional expertise was respected. It is interesting to note that two physicians could traditionally determine insanity without any special training in either psychiatry or psychology.

Finally, the era of extensive procedural due process was still ahead. The poor quite frequently went to court without lawyers and many things now determined by trials were determined more summarily. Again, the two-physician certificate usually sufficient to put a person involuntarily into a mental hospital is a good illustration.

It is important to distill an intervention rationale from this period. There appears to be a dearth of opinion that what was done was punitive or even simply expedient. It was instead based on a paternalistic model. The procedure was said to be in the best interests of the person named "patient" or "ward." It is a model under which we govern many affairs of our children. For the incompetent, it was thought to provide better property management and, for his/her mental condition, cure, improvement, or at least a less traumatic life setting. I have not found any serious empirical testing of the benefit assumptions made during this period.

II. The Present

The principal changes in guardianship from the recent past have been semantic. Insanity has given way to gradations of incompetency. A person is said to be incompetent for a specific purpose. Thus one can be said to be incompetent to stand trial and yet competent to manage finances. A few states attempt to identify specific functions which cannot competently be managed and to provide a surrogate for only those functions.

The legal concept insanity has almost totally been displaced by a mental equivalent such as mental illness, but very little has changed about the concept of responsibility, other than semantics. For example, when the insanity test was in vogue the testimony in cases appears to have been largely the same testimony that is now admitted on the issue of functional competence. Primarily, the question still is how abnormal the behavior of the person. Whether described in medical jargon or in lay language, judgment about behavior was and is the central test. One should not be surprised.

Precisely the same thing is true in criminal law. The insanity of a defendant is relevant to his or her responsibility. Functional competence to assist in one's defense is relevant to one's triability. If one compares the testimony introduced on the question of responsibility with the testimony introduced on competence to stand trial he/she will find the same similarity that is to be found in testimony concerning the need for the modern guardian as was applicable to guardianship in the past.

The change has taken place in an environment in which notions of psychiatric-psychological competence have changed drastically. Psychiatrists-psychologists are readily invited into court to discuss such traditional medical questions as prognosis for alleviation of medical conditions and such traditional factual questions as prediction of future dangerousness to self or others.

It is a hallmark of this period that psychiatrists-psychologists are assumed as competent to perform the second type of function as the first. In fact, they are far more commonly asked to court to perform that function than to perform the more traditional medical function. Incredibly, their ability to perform in this function was not seriously tested empirically until only relatively recently. Not surprisingly, the results of the test were devastating to psychiatrists-psychologists. They showed that psychiatrists-psychologists, as predictors of future conduct, were no better than nonmedical predictors, and that the pressures of the system made them significantly overpredict dangerousness.

While the concept of responsibility was undergoing semantic change and the notion of psychiatric-psychological competence was enhanced (the empirical studies have not yet changed that), the legal system at large dramatically changed its attitude about both civil and criminal due process. Prodded by strong decisions of the Warren Court, trial-like procedures were adopted in criminal as well as civil cases for many persons who had not previously had trials. Lawyers were provided in cases in which people had previously been unrepresented. Thinking that the Burger Court may have ended the period of aggressive growth of procedural due process, many bemoan the fact that procedures in the guardianship and commitment areas have not been sufficiently "fair," and bend their efforts toward providing more adversary processes. It is, in the trend of events, quite possible that they will succeed.

It is important to point out, however, that the due process thrust of many concerned with guardianship and commitment is misguided. What due process does is to insure that important determinations are made by careful focus on a precisely stated issue. What it cannot do is overcome the injustice of substantive law. In other words, due process is an appropriate safeguard if a fair substantive standard is applicable. At present, when notions as vague as incompetency prevail and medical testimony is taken as close to determinative, procedural due process obfuscates the problem by applying a fake patina of fairness.

Furthermore, the rationale for intervention has become considerably more muddled. There has been no repudiation of the paternalistic model. Proceedings are still justified as being in the best interests of the patient/client. But the contradictions have surfaced more than in the prior period. For example, one of the traditional reasons currently accepted for the appointment of a guardian is that the ward be unable to resist deception by artful or designing persons. At first blush, such a standard seems appropriate enough. One aspect of the ability to function is the ability to resist being overwhelmed by others. Further consideration suggests a deeper purpose. The language encourages a judge to focus on persons other than the proposed ward. Who? Daddy's young girlfriend? Mother's hairdresser? A new religious figure or charity? Surely, it is not the most direct way to focus on best interests of the ward. It may, however, be a good way to focus on the interests of those who would see the ward not dissipate his/her estate. That leads us to a closer examination of the intervention rationale in the present period.

With respect to surrogate property management, it is important to recognize that however benevolent the intention of those who would seek to substitute other decision makers for the aged, persons deprived of the right to decide for themselves will have lost the fairly basic attribute of citizenship. Consequently, it seems more appropriate to view the question of how the law should intervene, not as a question of maximizing benefit to the potential ward, but of reducing to a minimum the deprivation of the person's rights. From this perspective, one might better ask in whose interest is a surrogate manager of property appointed?

There is one sense in which the notion that the surrogate is imposed on an individual solely in his/her own interests is probably sound. It is doubtless true that courts could find property managers for most people who, because of superior experience and skill, would better manage the property than their wards. This is merely a specific application of the fact that there are usually people of greater skill and capacity than any given person. Without even considering whether the legal process is perfect enough to substitute a better decision maker in most cases, about which we could have some doubt, it is easy to reject the notion of benefit to a person occasioned by providing such paternalistic oversight. A person may, of course, always voluntarily obtain a skilled manager for his/her property; if one is involuntarily imposed on him/her, one should be skeptical of the benefit of such appointment to the potential ward.

Especially in the case of the aged, one can reject the facile answer often given in other cases that a surrogate can preserve property which his/her ward will later be able to use. To the extent that conditions of the aged are likely to be the result of general deterioration of mental processes, it seems unlikely that the property management function will often revert to the ward. Although wealth may increase, unless the ward retains the power to spend such money to maximize personal enjoyment, augmented affluence would hardly seem likely to be perceived by the ward as a benefit. It is, of course, possible that a condition requiring substitute management is temporary and that the ward will be able to benefit from an intervention which prevents the dissipation of property which later he/she could enjoy. At this point, the information available does not indicate what proportion of those enmeshed in surrogate management have a reasonable expectation of again becoming autonomous. The question should be explored.

Obviously, however, the ward is not only the person concerned in the maintenance of his/her wealth. Those who are potential beneficiaries of the ward's affluence feel a natural concern at its waste; the state has an interest in preventing its citizens from so reducing their financial integrity as to become public charges. What is important about these interests is that they are adverse to those of the ward. The present process, with its focus on benefit to the ward, inadequately and inarticulately deals with such interests.

In consequence, beneficiaries find themselves in the cynical position of being forced to plead in court for surrogate management premised on benefit to the object of the proceeding rather than, candidly, benefit to themselves. Unfortunately, when the underlying self-interest of the petitioner is probed, he/she appears in a very bad light in such court proceedings. Equally unfortunately, when this issue is not explored, potential beneficiaries may be awarded an interest in the ward's property which the court would find untenable were it determined from the perspective of protecting the beneficiaries' interest rather than the ward's.

Of course, avarice is not the only interest adverse to the interests of the ward. Persons may seek to have guardianship declared for administrative convenience. For this reason, apparently, the states of California and New York (two states I have studied) are active petitioners for guardianship of large numbers of people. Having the power to sign documents on behalf of their wards is obviously quite useful. A similar kind of utility may well attend to familial relations in the absence of an extensive estate.

Institutionalization, which is a normal though not necessary concomitant incident to the appointment of a guardian, may also provide convenience for persons other than the ward. While the sole alleged reason for institutionalizing a person has to do with that person's medical condition, it may mask the disinclination of relatives or of the state further to be burdened by the ward.

III. The Effect of Guardianship

Throughout this discussion it has been assumed that the principal reason for intervention in an older person's life is not danger to him or herself or others but rather because of debility. Consequently it seems appropriate to examine the extent to which intervention is helpful to that person in living out his or her life.

One study, while concluding that the most traumatic form of protective service was involuntary placement, attempted to discern the efficacy of all protective services, not just involuntary placement. The study went on to note, however, that service increases the likelihood of institutionalization: "(e)xperienced social workers appear to have a strong tendency to move old people into 'protective settings' when assigned responsibility for their welfare." The initial study found that, as to all protective services: "(o)ne must conclude on the basis of data gathered from following up. . .service and control cases the project service was not effective in slowing down deterioration and physical functioning—two major reasons frequently given for intervening in a protective case." The study's alarming conclusion was that protective services did not lengthen life. On the contrary, these services appeared to shorten people's lives.

The hypothesis was restudied and reconfirmed. At the conclusion of the second study the author (Benjamin Rose Institute, 1974) noted:

> Taking the findings as a whole it is difficult to avoid the conclusion that (a) participants in the experimental service program were institutionalized earlier than they would have otherwise been and (b) that this earlier institutionalization did not—contrary to intent—prove protective in terms of survival of the older person although it did relieve collaterals and community agents.

To understand why placement might prove so corrosive, it seems appropriate briefly to review some clinical evidence of the impact of involuntary commitment.

The aged are over-represented in the population of involuntary mental patients. Professor Regan (1972) has observed that "the percentage of mental hospital first admissions of elderly persons is increasing more rapidly than the total population of the aged" (p. 574) and that the aged make up 30 percent of mental hospital patients. It is unclear to what extent these statistics simply reflect increased debility in the aged. Also unknown is the number of patients who have nonpsychiatric medical problems. Unfortunately, as is true of much of

psychiatric diagnosis, nonpsychiatric diagnoses tend to reflect the expectations of those who bring patients to the diagnostician. "Dad is
just not himself." "Mom is so much more forgetful." "Dad's leg is
giving him so much more trouble." These and similar statements
provide a strong impression for a physician who may not have
previously seen the patient and who has had experience with patients
who were out of touch with their own functioning.

One of the most common diagnoses is acute or chronic brain
syndrome. Brain syndrome is considered acute if reversible and
chronic if otherwise. The disorder is typically thought to be an
organic dysfunction. Acute brain syndrome may, however, mask
such physical or mental conditions as simple depression, vitamin deficiency, traumatic injury, or a variety of other ills. If the underlying
condition is not treated, deterioration may in fact confirm the original
diagnosis of brain syndrome.

A brain syndrome diagnosis, in general, and certainly a chronic
brain syndrome diagnosis, in particular, may be a self-fulfilling
prophecy. In addition, the diagnosis may mask needed treatment in a
less dramatic way. For example, a colleague recently discussed a
situation in which his mother had suffered a stroke. She made a
miraculous recovery; all but bladder function returned to normal.
The treating physician was pleased, so pleased in fact that it did not
occur to him to investigate the cause of the remaining problem. At
my colleague's insistence, the physician eventually diagnosed the
condition. He found a massive infection which quickly responded to
treatment. The patient was cured of all symptoms.

Much of the initial data on which mental health diagnosticians
act in these cases concerns behavior. The symptomatology of brain
syndrome is that a previously healthy individual suddenly becomes
disturbed, confused, restless, or disoriented. Because a significant
portion of chronic brain syndrome diagnosis is comparative, data
must be matched against the patient's prior mental history. Most of
the behavioral symptoms on which a decision must be made will
already have taken place by the time the physician sees the patient.
Therefore, heavy reliance must be placed on an informant's observation of the person's conduct. The opportunity for bias on the informant's part is obvious. Just as an incompetency proceeding can be
used to indicate the petitioner's interest in the finances of an older
person, so too can information about the older person's behavior be

used to cast him or her as sufficiently debilitated to require involuntary treatment.

I do not suggest that the informant must necessarily be conscious of his/her role, or must necessarily be lying. The entire inquiry is sufficiently unclear that it is possible to paint a picture of gross disability simply by the selective recollections, however innocent, of recent events. The diagnosis in turn relects the same vague standards. Wang (1969) reports that 77.7 percent of first time geriatric admissions in the year he studied were admitted for brain syndrome. Another study of diagnoses of patients over sixty-five on first admissions to mental hospitals in Toronto, New York, and London found the respective percentages to be 41.8 percent in Canada, 79.8 percent in New York, and 42.8 percent in England. The study concluded that the difference in percentages was probably not the result of differences in patients, but rather differences in the diagnostic bias of United States physicians. In Canada and England, the percentages of functional (nonorganic) disorders were comparably higher. Because there is wide textbook difference between nonorganic dysfunction and organic brain syndrome, these discrepancies indicate some reason for skepticism about chronic brain syndrome diagnoses.

Apparently the early experience in California under Lanterman-Petris-Short confirms this belief. One group (ENKI Research Institute, 1972) has noted,

> Some mentally disordered patients were placed involuntarily in locked facilities under the diagnosis of chronic brain syndrome and were not provided the opportunity for judicial review of the involuntary hold. The locked facilities licensed by the state DMH (California Department of Mental Health) were generally used to provide care for the geriatric, senile patient who would otherwise wander out into the community, and needed a protective setting to prevent harm from coming to him because of his condition of incompetency. The diagnosis of chronic brain syndrome was considered to be an irreversible condition from which the patient would not 'clear' or improve. In actual practice, some patients so placed in these facilities with a diagnosis of chronic brain syndrome became 'clear', and did improve. A number of professional persons were concerned that the mentally

disordered were being place in locked facilities and forgotten rather than being placed in a protective, *but not locked* facility such as a board-and-care home. (p. 159)

IV. The End of the Present System

It appears that the tensions that exist among competing concepts have begun to destroy the present system. Such an overthrow does present many positive aspects and should be encouraged. It is difficult to assess change in its midst but I believe change is almost upon us.

One cannot, for example, overlook the work of the National Senior Citizens Center which did a study of the California conservatorship law and found that 80 percent of the persons for whom conservatorship had been ordered were over sixty-five. In addition, they found that 93 percent of those people had been conserved without their appearance in court. Finally they noted that 97 percent had been conserved without legal representation in the proceedings. Incidentally, substantive provisions of California law require appearance in court except for medical excuse and provide for counsel.

How then is it possible that substantive law is so largely disregarded? In my judgment that has to do with the professional competence consideration referred to earlier. Both lawyers and psychiatrists have been co-opted by the idea that psychiatric prediction of future conduct is reliable. Not only have psychiatrists undertaken to testify to future conduct but lawyers have begun, in large numbers, to act as though they also had an appropriate role to play in predicting future conduct (with or without the help of psychiatrists-psychologists).

Thus it has become possible for everyone in the system to adopt a paternalistic model and obtain a guardianship for a person "in need" using legal skills principally to prevent the "traumatic" intervention of legal process. Wards are not in court because physicians are found who will sign certificates that court appearance would be psychologically devastating. Wards are not represented by independent counsel because petitioning counsel is seen as acting in the best interests of the ward.

No study was as helpful in this effort to obtain the new California conservatorship law as this one. The reaction to it suggests that at least at the intuitive level, the interventionist rationale may be rejected by the public.

Another illustration of the present system coming under stress is to be found in the trend of new legislation. It has rapidly moved from allowing open-ended intervention to requiring that intervention be for fixed periods of time. The best illustration comes from California's Lanterman-Petris-Short Act (which is not a guardianship law at all but the law relating to involuntary hospitalization). In it, except for persons theoretically totally unable to function, the so-called "gravely disabled," all involuntary commitments are made for very short periods of time. Procedures are provided for extending those periods of time through court proceedings but these extending procedures are very rarely used. Furthermore, initial empirical study suggests that short-term intervention is no less effective than the prior indefinite intervention. If future studies confirm the initial results, it will probably become much more difficult to justify long-term intervention.

Finally, the Lanterman-Petris-Short Act also shows the extent to which the competence issue has become distorted. Under Lanterman-Petris-Short the selection of persons for inclusion in the mental health system is made by legal authority (lawyers or law enforcement personnel, generally). It is up to them to decide whether the person is to be processed as a patient, or, assuming socially unacceptable behavior, as a criminal. Under Lanterman-Petris-Short it then becomes the physician's responsibility to focus on the issues of danger to self and danger to others both in the present (required by the statute) and in the near future.

In other words, the issue of treatability (the only issue physicians are trained to handle well) is handled by law-trained people. The issue of conduct (the issue that law-trained people normally handle well) is handled by physicians.

V. The Near Term

If the present system fails, alternatives should be available. Given present concepts relating to responsibility, competence, and due process, it seems to me that any viable new system will not be very different from the one at hand. A few modest proposals follow as suggestions as to what could probably be accommodated in such a minor revision.

The first proposal is that the law be rewritten to eliminate vindication of adverse interests. If, for example, there are persons who have a legitimate concern about inheriting from an older person who is currently squandering money, the law should either recognize that interest (as it does the interest of a creditor in debt payment, a property holder of a remainder interest in preventing waste by the current tenant, a wife in postmarital support, the state in having its tax bills paid) or should recognize that it does not recognize them. In any event, all people having an interest should be allowed to protect their interest to the extent that, for example, creditors currently protect their interest through legal proceedings. No one would be required to go to court to talk about the best interests of their debtor.

Second, and closely related, the law could be written to take out all financial incentives for bringing proceedings. It will always be difficult to test the extent to which avarice has played a part in bringing proceedings. Equally, administrative sloth has made states large-scale petitioners. Perhaps, for some time, we should try disincentives in law, making dealing with wards even more burdensome to administrators and making devolution of property even more difficult for beneficiaries than under present interstate succession. I don't propose to draft that law now but simply suggest that it seems to me to be a law that can be drafted using available legal constructs.

Third, and perhaps more important, the limited competence that is available to society through both lawyers and physicians should be applied in a reordered fashion to maximize its benefit. Lawyers should be absolutely prohibited (I believe that a proper interpretation of ethical considerations already prohibits them) from undertaking to represent a person and then, later, petitioning for anyone's involuntary intervention in his/her client's affairs. If there are people to deal with involuntary intervention, they should be people trained in social work, psychology, psychiatry, or some similar field. Since psychiatrists have difficulty knowing when to resort to involuntary process, lawlyers should certainly not attempt the task.

Finally, the law should limit psychiatrists-psychologists to dealing with the issue they can address best: treatability. No reason appears why anyone not treatable should ever be hospitalized. Furthermore, no reason suggests itself why a physician ought ever to be involved in the question of a person's ability to function in property management or determinations of danger to society or related fields since those issues are issues that are similar to other questions of fact with which lawyers customarily deal.

The most difficult question that would not be resolved by simply assigning to the two principal professions the areas they handle best arises out of our present concern for responsibility. What is to be done with the "irresponsible person" who may resist treatment or surrogate property management as part of the mental condition for which we would hold him/her irresponsible? The question does not allow an easy answer that is socially acceptable. My answer would be that the best *available* way of dealing with the problem is to accept what a person says whether we consider the person competent or incompetent in other respects. Since I recognize that solution to be out of line with current notions I have a modest proposal that may be more acceptable: Every person would still be the ultimate judge of whether intervention is to take place in his/her life. The test would become "what would the person have done if competent to decide?" The idea is not a new one.

Several states have recently adopted laws that allow people to direct that their life not be artificially maintained when survival becomes impossible and when they can no longer be consulted. It is only a short step from such a declaration to a further declaration respecting what to do if, in the future, a person was found to be incompetent to make contemporary decisions. Some will no doubt choose to authorize intervention. In fact, such authorization statements are already in limited use. Others will certainly choose to reject such intervention.

To keep legal issues to a minimum, a statement as to future desire should probably become incontestable after a year or two. Otherwise one would always have to go back to the question of whether the person was competent to make the original statement. I think society can live with a system in which a person who has not been in a psychiatric hospital for say a year or so can have his/her written wishes honored as to whether now to hospitalize. Similarly, wishes with respect to surrogate management of property can be honored.

Of course, most persons will not execute a statement either for or against involuntary intervention. Even for them, however, it seems to me the question of what they would have requested had they made a statement is the best available issue on which to determine intervention. The issue of what a person would have done is clearly a legal (not a medical) issue. Lawyers can presumably focus on conduct evidencing a desire for help or rejecting medical treatment in other contexts. As far as hospitalization is concerned, physicians would then have the opportunity to determine whether they can be of benefit should the person be hospitalized. Both groups would do what they do best.

VI. The Future

Several future events will require radical reconsideration of guardianship. For example, a drug has just appeared on the market which purports to improve memory for older people. Such medical advances are bound to continue. It may well be that other advances in medicine may make restoration to full function so desirable, and the coercive aspects of psychiatric treatment of the present so unnecessary, as to dissolve the issue of forced treatment. We don't currently have a coercive system to administer penicillin, for example. The same is true of property management. If alternatives to self-management become attractive enough, they may well become routine.

Secondly, we may find some inventive way to get in touch with a person's intention without the distortion that emotional problems may bring. It is difficult, for the moment, to suggest quite how that might happen. But it could. That would again make a dramatic change, since the principal reason for treating wards differently is the assumption that they can no longer exercise the autonomous choice guaranteed to the rest of us.

Finally, and for me most ominously, there will probably come a time when the prediction of future conduct becomes quite reliable. I should not be surprised to find such a breakthrough coming from chemistry or electronics rather than psychiatry. But it could come from anywhere. What then? I am not prepared to begin to answer that question, except to say that all of society's course of intervention in the criminal, juvenile, and mental health systems would have to be radically re-examined, since all are equally premised on the inability to be certain about the future.

REFERENCES

Aldrich, C.K., & Mendkoff, E. Relocation of the aged & disabled: A morality study. *Journal of American Geriatric Society,* 1963 *11,* 185.

Alexander, G.J. On being imposed upon by artful or designing persons—The California experience with the involuntary placement of the aged. *San Diego Law Review,* 1977 *14,* 1083.

American Bar Association, Commission on the Mentally Disabled, Developmental Disabilities State Leg. Project. *Guardianship and conservatorship* (a survey of guardianship—conservatorship statutes), 1979.

Benjamin Rose Institute. *Progress report on protective services for older people,* 1967, 68-69.

————. Protective services for older people: Findings from the Benjamin Rose Institute Study, 1974, 157.

Blenkner, M. Environmental change and the aging individual. *Gerontologist, 1967 7,* 101.

Busse, E.W. Mental disorder in later life—Organic brain syndome. In E. Basse & E. Pfeiffer, *Mental Illness in Later Life,* 1973, 89.

Butler, R. N. *Why survive?* New York: Harper & Row, 1975. Psychiatry and the elderly: An overview. *American Journal of Psychiatry,* Sept. 1975, 132, 893.

California Welfare & Institution Code SS SS 5000—5404.1 (West 1972 & Supp. 1979) (Lanterman-Petris-Short Act).

Cohen, G. D. Approach to the geriatric patient. *Medical Clinics of N. America,* 1977, 855.

Dershowitz, A. Psychiatry in the legal process: A knife that cuts both ways. *Trial,* 1968, *4,* 29.

Developments in the law—Civil commitment of the mentally ill. *Harvard Law Review,* 1974 *87,* 1190.

Duckworth, G.S. & Ross, A. Diagnostic differences in

psychogeriatric patients in Toronto, New York, and London, England. *Canadian Medical A. Journal,* 1975 *122,* 847.

ENKI Research Institute, *A study of California's new mental health law,* 1972.

Ennis, B.J., & Litwack, T.R. Psychiatry and the presumption of expertise: Flipping coins in the courtroom. *California Law Review,* 1974 *62,* 693.

Gaylin, W., Glasser, I., Marcus, S., Rothman, D. *Doing good,* 1978.

Goldfarb, W., Memory & Aging. In R. Goldman & M. Rockstein (Eds.) *Physiology and Pathology of Human Aging,* 1975 *149.*

Horstman, P.M. Protective services for the elderly: the limits of parens patriae. *Mo. Law Review,* 1975 *40,* 191.

Langer, E.J. & Rodin, J. The effects of choice and enhanced personal responsibility for the aged: a field experiment in an institutional setting. *Journal of Personality & Social Psychology,* 1976 *34,* 191.

Leifer, R. The competence of the psychiatrist to assist in the determination of incompetency: A skeptical inquiry into the courtroom functions of psychiatrists. *Syracuse Law Review* 1961 *14,* 564.

Lewin, T. *The aged and the need for surrogate management.* Syracuse: Syracuse University, 1972.

Lieberman, M.A. Relationship of mortality rates to entrance for a home for the aged. *Geriatrics,* 1961 *16,* 515.

Mental Disability. *L. Rep.* 1979, *3,* 106-14. (survey of state laws governing civil commitment).

National Institute of Aging, National Institutes of Health. *Treatable Dementia in the Elderly,* 1978.

The National Senior Citizens Center is a federally funded legal service center concerned with the legal problems of the elderly poor. The study cited was an empirical study covering the complete Los Angeles County central district guardianship and conservatorship filings under Cal. Prob. Code SS 1460—1470 (West 1956) and Cal. Prob. Code SS 1701—2207 (West Supp. 1977) from July 1, 1973–June 30, 1974. One thousand ten case files were examined.

Plotkin, R. Limiting the therapeutic orgy: Mental patient's right to refuse treatment. *Nw. U. Law Review 1978 72,* 461.

Premature probate: A different perspective on guardianship for the elderly. *Stanford Law Review,* 1979 *31,* 1003.

President's Commission on Mental Health. *Report of the Task Panel on the Mental Health of the Elderly*, 1978, 1131.

Regan, J.J. Protective services for the elderly: Commitment, guardian-ship, and alternatives. *William & Mary Law Review* 1972 *13*, 569, 588–589.

Rohan, P.J. Caring for persons under a disability: A critique of the role of the conservator and the substitution of judgment doctrine. *St. John's Law Review*, 1977 *52*, 1.

Subcommittee on health and long-term care, house select comm. on aging. New Perspectives in Health Care for Older Americans, Comm. Print 1976.

Szasz, T. *The myth of mental illness* (2nd ed.) New York: Harper & Row 1974. *Ideology and insanity* 1970 & Alexander, G.J. Law, property and psychiatry. *American Journal of Ortho-Psychiatry*, 1972 *42*, 610.

Wang, H.S. Organic brain syndromes. In E. Busse & E. Pfeiffer, (eds.). *Behavior and Adaptation in Later Life*, 1969 *263*, 265.

A number of states have statutes providing for court appointment of a guardian or conservator on a voluntary request by an aged person. E. G. Cal. Porb. Code & 1751 (West Supp. 1979); Iowa Code Ann. SS 633.572 (Supp. 1979-80); Kan. Stat. Ann. SS 59-3007 (1976); Okla. Stat. Ann. Tit. 58 SS 890.1 (Supp. 1979-80).

Chapter 6

SOCIETAL ATTITUDES AND ETHICAL CHOICES IN HEALTH CARE OF THE ELDERLY

Margaret J. Kustaborder

Individuals are socialized first by their families and later by various professionals, all part of the larger culture. The values and beliefs of this larger culture influence all individual behavior including that of health care givers, often at a subconscious level. Our society teaches that growing old is bad and to be avoided as long as possible. We learn that all old people must be looked after, are childish, senile, irritable, incapable of reasoning, incapable of learning new information, and incapable of making intelligent decisions about their own lives. These unfounded societal attitudes influence the quality of health care provided for the elderly patient, even the quality of care given by nurses.

If the nurse believes all old people are senile, increasing confusion in an older patient will not be noticed and the cause of the confusion will not be investigated. A seventy-four year old woman had hip surgery. She complained of weakness and became more confused with each postoperative day. Her nurses were asked for information about the onset of this confusion. They reported that they didn't know, probably a long time; the patient was old and senile. When the patient's husband was asked the same question, he said, ''Only since her surgery last week. She drives the car, shops for groceries, everything. I am concerned about the confusion and her weakness. It's just not like her to complain every time they get her out of bed.'' The physician was provided with this information along with a request for blood studies. The patient had a hemaglobin of 8 grams. After two blood transfusions, her confusion disappeared and the patient was looking forward to getting well and going home.

If the nurse believes that body image is not important to the elderly because, after all, they are old and wrinkled and gray, who will remember to offer assistance with make-up for women or daily shaves for men? Who will find time to listen to the feelings of the seventy-nine-year-old woman who has had a mastectomy, and certainly who will think of this woman's need for a prosthesis (Carnevali & Patrick, 1979). Yet if these patients become quiet and refuse to see certain visitors, this same nurse will label them as uncooperative or depressed.

If the nurse believes that all old people are like children, the patient's dignity and self-esteem are disregarded. He/she will not be properly covered during a bed bath, the bathroom door will be left open or the curtains not drawn around the bed when he/she is using the bedpan. This nurse will arrange the female patients' hair in long braids or "pompoms" and tie big ribbons on the ends. The patients will be addressed as "honey" or "dear" or by their first names, never respectfully as Mr. Jones or Mrs. Smith.

Because this nurse believes old people are childish, the patient's personal effects may be searched "for his own good." One nursing home resident, with a medical diagnosis of adult onset diabetes, received a 1000 calorie ADA diet. She got very hungry for sweets, phoned her friendly drug store, and had them deliver some hard candy. She kept the candy in her purse and ate a piece on occasion. The nursing staff raided her purse and removed the candy adding that she was "a bad girl and should have known better." The patient got very angry and used about the only means available to her to protest effectively: she urinated on the floor beside her bed every night. A clinical specialist was consulted by the staff to help solve the problem of this patient's incontinence. The consultant listened to the patient. With the approval of the physician and dietician, the patient was served a piece of pie each Sunday, and the nursing staff sat down and visited with her for 10 minutes on each shift. She no longer ordered candy and she stopped urinating on the floor.

If the nurse believes all old people are deaf, communication will be very loud and often abrasive. A seventy-seven year-old woman fell and was taken to the Emergency Room by her daughter. The E.R. nurse asked her the necessary questions in a very loud voice and then went to get the doctor. The patient expressed concern for the nurse, that she was so young and so deaf. Her daughter had to explain that the young nurse could hear and that it was she, the patient, who was supposed to be deaf.

If the nurse believes that older people are incapable of learning new information, less time will be spent in teaching the patient about health, disease, or coping behaviors (Carnevali & Patrick, 1979). If the nurse believes a patient can learn, has knowledge of and understands the aging process, then time will be taken to find out what the patient does know, what he/she wants to learn, and a teaching plan will be developed to meet these needs.

If the nurse believes the adult children of aged parents should assume parenting or executor roles, important decisions will be discussed with the children, rather than the patient (Carnevali & Patrick, 1979). Very often the middle-aged children know more about the health problem of the patient than does the patient himself. Many elderly have been shipped off to nursing homes because the adult children listened to the social worker, nurse, or physician and were convinced their parent could not return to the community and independent living. Often, the patient was not included in these discussions which influenced the quality of his/her life.

What can be done to change these beliefs that negatively affect the health care provided for the elderly? The answer, of course, is to change the attitude of society toward growing old, which is in itself a monumental task. A more attainable solution is to change the beliefs and improve the attitudes of health-care providers toward the elderly.

All nursing staff (RN, LPN, NA) should be taught the basic physiologic aging process while relating the aging changes to nursing needs of the elderly patients. Discussing the aging process in relation to the health needs of young nursing staff, to prepare them for a healthier old age, quietly reminds the staff that they too will someday reach old age. Considerable time should be spent discussing the psychosocial problems of aging such as retirement, loss of income, family and health. Special emphasis should be placed on the well elderly, the 95 percent of our older citizens who live out in the community exhibiting tremendous adaptation and coping abilities. Anyone who has lived seventy, eighty, or ninety years and successfully coped with all of life's challenges is worthy of admiration.

One method of educating the staff and changing their societal attitudes toward aging is the use of small workshops in which the participants are encouraged to look at their own feelings about loss and death (Wylie & Kustaborder, 1979). These workshops were successful in effecting a change in the staff's attitude toward elderly patients, as well as a change in attitude toward each other. The staff became more caring in a positive, productive way. They appeared to be more sensitive to the needs of others.

When elderly patients are admitted to a hospital, everything the nursing staff does to or for the patient encourages dependence. The patient is told when to bathe, sleep, go to physical therapy, and take medications. The patient is not allowed to assume responsibility for his/her health even though he/she must assume this responsibility if he/she is ever to live independently again. For many years nursing leaders have encouraged nurses to include the patient when planning patient care. For some nurses, this is difficult to do. Nurses know that patients have rights, but they have planned patient care for so long without assistance that they really do not know how to include the patient. Staff nurses need help with this process, they need role models to observe and follow. Nursing instructors should work closely with students when planning patient care so that the students know how to include the patient in care planning when they become practitioners. If the nurse and patient identify problems and plan together, they will certainly get to know each other better, and this too would help to change attitudes. It would also lead to better compliance with prescribed treatments, medications, and diet by the patient.

Changing the attitudes about aging held by all health care providers could be a lengthy process. If schools of nursing, medicine, and social work would include gerontology as part of the curriculum, the process could be shortened. Knowledge does not necessarily lead to a change in attitude, but it does eliminate myths and misconceptions.

Required studies of the social sciences or courses in the humanities by students in the health professions might lead to a better understanding of the dimensions of human existence and to more caring attitudes (Carper, 1979).

If we profess to believe in the dignity and worth of our elderly patients, Levine (1977) observes, "It should be agreed that the wholeness which is part of our awareness of ourselves is shared best with others when no act diminishes another person and no moment of indifference leaves him with less of himself'' (p. 849).

REFERENCES

Carnevali, D., & Patrick, M. *Nursing management for the elderly*. Philadelphia: J. B. Lippincott Co., 1979.

Carper, B. The ethics of caring. *Advances in Nursing Science*, Aspen Systems Corporation, April 1979, pp. 11-19.

Levine, M. Nursing ethics and the ethical nurse. *American Journal of Nursing*, May 1977, pp. 845-849.

Wylie, N., & Kustaborder, M. Helping care givers cope with loss, especially dying. Submitted for publication 1979.

Chapter 7

THE ETHICS OF SUICIDE IN OLD AGE

Harry R. Moody

At the time that Socrates drank the hemlock and took his own life, he offered as one of the reasons for his action the fact that he was now old (age seventy) and had lived a full and rich life. At that age, Socrates felt, was it not reasonable to accept an end to his life rather than face alternatives such as disobedience to civil law or disgrace in exile? The Socratic question was later refined by the Stoic philosophers who argued that the ultimate criterion of the good life was quality, not quantity of life. In old age, then, "natural death" was entirely appropriate and even a self-inflicted death could be a truly rational decision. Thus, with Socrates and the Stoic philosophers, in the earliest centuries of the Western philosophical tradition, rational suicide on grounds of old age appears as a subject of ethical debate.

Today the ethical debate still continues. Current experience in the field of aging leaves no doubt that the problem of suicide in old age is a vexing one. Psychiatrists, social workers, nurses, and other professionals are often confused about what their response should be. Should suicide among the elderly be seen as a symptom of depression and, therefore, treated in order to cure or prevent it? Or, conversely, do we have an obligation to guarantee each individual a "death with dignity" that might mean the choice to end one's own life? There is considerable philosophical and practical dispute about these questions. Even if we do not share Albert Camus' view that suicide is the *only* serious philosophical problem, we still must agree that our ethical view of rational suicide becomes, quite literally, a life-and-death matter. Do we intervene to prevent or go forward to facilitate a person's decision to die? The wrong answer to this question risks enormous injustice. Yet most of us find ourselves torn.

Definition of the Problem.

First, it is necessary to be as clear as possible about what precisely is the meaning of the question, "Is suicide on grounds of old age ethically justified?" We are concerned here with the act of *suicide* in the strong sense of the term: that is, with intentional acts of self-killing, not with "allowing to die" or other indirect circumstances having consequences that may end life. Second, we are concerned with the choice of suicide *on grounds of* old age, not simply in the period of old age or as a result of a life-threatening or terminal illness. We are *not* concerned with all the questions typically treated in the bioethical literature on euthanasia.

It is also important to consider whether suicide on grounds of old age can be *ethically* justified. We are *not* concerned with its *legal* permissibility, which may vary according to legal codes and the chances of enforcement of those codes. Suppose, then, we acknowledge, at least for the sake of argument, that there ought to be a legal *right* to commit suicide: that is, suicide, among the elderly or any other group, ought not be subject to sanctions of criminal law. We might extend this point to eliminate laws prohibiting assisting a suicide, making efforts to safeguard against disguised homicides or other self-interested promotion of suicide among the elderly, e.g., on grounds of inheritance. Even if we were successfully to implement such safeguards and such a legal "right" to suicide, ethical problems would remain. Accepting suicide as a legal right does *not* imply that it is an ethically justified course of action. As Dworkin (1977) observes,

> The word 'right' has different force in different contexts. . .
> e.g., you have the right to spend money gambling, if you wish,
> though you ought to spend it in a more worthwhile way. . .
> There is a clear difference between saying that someone

has a right to do something in this sense and saying that it is
the 'right' thing for him to do, or that he does no wrong in
doing it. Someone may have the right to do something that is
the wrong thing for him to do (e.g., gambling) (p. 188).

Suicide, then, may be both a legal and a moral right, yet still not be the
right thing for a person to do on some specific grounds, e.g., old age.

Arguments against Suicide

In order to take the ethical question seriously, we must assume that
suicide itself can be a rational option: that is, a serious life choice, the outcome of a process of intelligent deliberation. We must assume, in other
words, that suicide, at least in some cases, is a free action in the simple
sense that the agent "could have done otherwise." To say that suicide
can be rational does not suggest that it is a good decision but just that it is
a free choice. In the same sense, we can describe a person planning a
bank robbery as engaged in a rational decision. He may be mistaken,
may be acting unethically, but at least the action is his own and fulfills the
conditions of freedom and rationality required for ethical choice.

This point is crucial to our argument, since professionals in the field
of aging often assume that acts of suicide in old age are forms of depression or "mental illness." This presumption of irrationality is of the
ideology of the mental health profession concerned with suicide
prevention. A problem arises here because of a contraindication between two of our cherished beliefs: first, that society has no business in-
terfering with free, private decisions ("self-regarding" decisions, as
John Stuart Mill would have put it); and, second, that killing oneself
is a bad thing, indeed an irreversible evil that should by all means be
prevented. This conflict between the libertarian and welfare perspectives is troublesome. We find it possible to reconcile the two points of
view by concluding that anyone who decides to kill him or herself isn't
really free: that is, by deciding that a choice of suicide is, prima facie, a
sign of mental illness.

As a rule, the claim that suicide demonstrates mental illness doesn't
even require proof; it is taken for granted. In this circular logic, suicide is
a sure sign of mental illness because only people who are crazy
("pathologically depressed") would try to kill themselves. From this
assumption follows the rationale for suicide prevention programs. Yes,

people have a perfect right to kill themselves but if they try to exercise that right, it proves that they aren't really free and rational agents, so they need treatment for their emotional disorder. If they are treated and still decide to kill themselves, well, that simply shows the treatment wasn't successful.

Suicide in Old Age: A Reasonable Alternative

The ideology of suicide prevention, whatever its psychological underpinnings, essentially expresses a common-sense belief that life is a good thing and that it is better to live than to die. In cases of attempted suicides who are young or middle-aged, it is easy to produce plausible arguments for suicide prevention:

(1) The person attempting suicide very likely has external obligations — if not financial dependents, then at least people who would be affected emotionally by the act of suicide ("No man is an island").

(2) The state of mind leading to suicide may be only temporary. People often change their minds, provided only that they are alive in the future to do so.

(3) Even if circumstances are bad now, no one can predict the future. Things may get better.

(4) Suicide in youth or middle age is a violent disturbance of the "natural life cycle," depriving the individual of a full life.

Only the first of these arguments is based on the moral force of duties to other people. The last three turn on some concept of "duty to oneself" (whatever this may mean), which amounts to a claim that the person attempting suicide, on rational grounds, has misconstrued his or her own best interests.

Regardless of whether these arguments for suicide prevention work for other age groups, in the case of old age none of them seem to work.

(1) *Deliberate Choice.* The aged person who chooses suicide after years of reflection and deliberation (not a temporary disposition) expresses fundamental value judgments, not a momentary mental state.

(2) *Negative Future Outlook.* While the future may be unpredictable in youth, advanced age has a predictable outcome: limited life expec-

tancy, with the likelihood of diminished quality of life and irreparable losses of meaning or happiness.

(3) *Disengagement*. Old age is often a period of disengagement by successful withdrawal from external obligations and relationships. With retirement and children moving away, with the death of friends and relatives, fewer and fewer interpersonal obligations remain. In many cases, there is no one left to be negatively affected by one's death.

(4) *Natural Death*. With advanced old age, people have lived out a "natural" lifespan of three score years and ten or many more. When an aged person dies we usually do not feel that their death is "premature" or "unfair." Indeed, the prototype of a natural death is death in old age, which may well be brought about by personal decision.

We can summarize the situation by the following question. What objection can there possibly be to the decision of an old person, who has lived a full life, whose external obligations are fulfilled, who faces the prospect of infirmity and decline, and who rationally and deliberately chooses suicide as the form of death? Could this choice of suicide not only be a *right*, but in fact be the *right thing* to do? This question sharpens the sense in which rational suicide on grounds of old age might be ethically justified. To examine the validity of the argument let us look at two case studies that pose the issue sharply.

Karl Marx's Daughter (Choron, 1972).

The joint suicide of Karl Marx's daughter and her husband, Dr. Paul Lafargue, took place in 1911. The gardener discovered their bodies in a room off the garden of their home in Paris. "He was lying fully dressed on a bed; she was in an easy chair in an adjoining room. Before committing suicide Dr. Lafargue had written out a reference for his domestic help, signed his will, and even drafted the text of a telegram to be sent to his nephew (announcing their deaths)."

In his suicide note to friends Lafargue said:

"Sound of mind and body, I am killing myself before pitiless old age, which gradually deprives me of the pleasures and joys of existence and saps my physical and intellectual forces, will paralyze my energy, break my will power, and turn me into a burden to myself and others. Long ago I have promised myself not to live beyond the age of seventy. I have fixed the moment for my departure from life and I have prepared the method of executing my project: a hypodermic injection of hydrocyanic acid'' (p. 100).

Analysis of the Case. The case of Marx's daughter is a paradigm of what has been called the "balance sheet" argument favoring suicide on grounds of old age. When the balance of pain over pleasure in the years remaining becomes unfavorable, then the rational hedonist must properly decide for ending life. Note that there need not be any terminal or life-threatening illness to prompt the decision. An unfavorable "balance sheet" in old age might very well be a good reason. This sentiment is well expressed by comments quoted by John Fisher in an article cited by Doris Portwood (1978) in her book *Common-Sense Suicide: The Final Right*:

> I want to go while I can still enjoy my friends who are so good to me and who I know can still enjoy me. . . while I can still feel a not too unfavorable balance between happiness and competence and interest and even limited usefulness of my days— and the difficulties and discomforts and pain and expense involved in trying first to maintain that balance and then later merely to prolong my life (p. 32).

We should note, too, here the tendency for the pure egotist or hedonist standpoint of the "balance sheet" to merge with what is essentially a utilitarian argument. Suicide on grounds of old age, in other words, might not be merely a matter of self-determination but even an obligation to the greater welfare of society. Portwood, for example, takes this balance-sheet utilitarianism to its logical extreme:

> The suicide of a nonproductive person with failing health is an entry for the other side of (the) public balance sheet. Her, or his, departure can hardly fail to be an asset for the com-

munity. If the suicide was a solvent taxpayer, taxes will be levied on the estate; if indigent, the government is spared further expense on a life basically finished (p. 44).

Portwood waxes enthusiastic over the utilitarian benefits of promoting rational suicide for the elderly, the main purpose of her book. She argues that popularizing old-age suicide might provide competition for dismal nursing homes (with a painless and peaceful death as the alternative) and in any event there would be a "fringe benefit" of donation of useful vital organs for transplantation. These macabre conclusions ought to make us question the premise underlying the entire argument for balance sheet suicide.

A decisive argument against the balance sheet suicide in old age is given by Immanual Kant (1964) in his *Foundations of the Metaphysics of Morals* and in other places in his writings on ethics. Kant's argument comes down to a version that he terms the "categorical imperative," sometimes interpreted as a version of the Golden Rule or principle of universal ethical obligation. In brief, this Kantian principle holds that the human being, as a free, moral being, has the status of an infinite or absolute value in the universe. All particular ethical injunctions flow from this fundamental principle of treating man with the respect deserved by such a being who is an end in himself. In Kant's formulation, this form of the categorical (or absolute) imperative goes as follows:

> So act as to treat humanity, whether in your own person or in that of any other, always at the same time as an end, and never merely as a means (p. 96).

Consistent with the supreme principle of moral law, Kant rejects the balance sheet argument for suicide:

> . . .the man who contemplates suicide will ask "Can my action be compatible with the idea of humanity as an end in itself?" If he does away with himself in order to escape from a painful situation, he is making use of a person merely as a means to maintain a tolerable state of affairs till the end of his life. But man is not a thing— not something to be used merely as a means: he must always in all his actions be regarded

as an end in himself. Hence I cannot dispose of man in my
person by maiming, spoiling, or killing (p. 97).

The balance sheet argument makes the balance of pleasure and
pain the final criterion for whether human life is worth living, on
either selfish grounds (my private balance sheet) or on altruistic-
utilitarian grounds— the fear of being a burden to others. If we accept the altruistic version of the balance sheet argument, then the
logic of utilitarianism may lead to the point where the welfare of
society makes suicide in old age not merely permissible but obligatory
in order to bring about the greatest happiness for the greatest
number.

It is this line of thought— whether hedonism or utilitarianism—
that Kant rejects entirely by his concept of man as an end in himself.
H.J. Paton (1958) has argued that the Kantian ethic would affirm a
right to commit suicide only in the case where there is no further
possibility of living a moral life and exhibiting those capabilities of
human nature that define man's ultimate moral worth. Suicide
undertaken to avoid the decline and infirmity of old age put limits on
the dignity of the human being in the name of empirically contingent
factors of happiness. If man, by contrast, is a moral personality and
an end in himself, then he retains this intrinsic and infinite worth
even in advanced old age.

The Quality-of-Life Argument

Kant's argument against balance sheet suicide leaves open a
loophole that might support rational suicide on grounds of old age in
just those cases when there is no further possibility of living a moral
life (in Kant's sense). In cases where quality-of-life falls below some
unacceptable standard, would rational suicide then be justifiable?
The following case underscores this quality-of-life argument favoring
suicide in old age:

The Van Dusen Case

In 1975, Dr. and Mrs. Henry Van Dusen, aged 77 and 80
respectively, attempted suicide by taking an overdose of
sleeping pills. Mrs. Van Dusen died immediately. Dr. Van

Dusen survived but died two weeks later of a heart ailment. The Van Dusens were well-known figures in American religion. Before his retirement, Dr. Van Dusen had been President of Union Theological Seminary and a prominent ecumenical leader. The couple's decision to commit suicide was evidently the result of a long and thoughtful reflection. Both Van Dusens were members of the Euthanasia Society and, according to the *New York Times* report, "had entered into the (suicide) pact rather than face the prospect of debilitating old age." In the suicide note left by them they explicitly vowed that they would not "die in a nursing home." Both Van Dusens suffered from chronic health problems: she from arthritis, he from the effects of a stroke that interfered with normal speech. The *Times* report noted that "For the vigorous articulate Presbyterian scholar and his active wife, the setbacks were serious impediments to living the kind of useful, productive lives to which they had become accustomed" (pp. 1, 43).

The Van Dusen case is a vivid one and was much publicized at the time, but the reasoning behind the Van Dusens' decision has an ancient and venerable history. As Socrates replied in the dialogue *Crito* when he was asked if he did not have a duty to save his own life by escaping: "The point, my dear Crito, is not simply to live, but to live well," he replied. This theme is taken up by Stoics, especially in the writings of the Roman philosopher Seneca, an articulate defender of rational suicide.

Seneca argues that the wise man ought to choose suicide well before a terminal illness threatens the quality of life:

(The wise man) holds that it makes no difference to him whether his taking-off be natural or self-inflicted. He does not regard it with fear, as if it were a great loss; for no man can lose very much when but a driblet remains. It is not a question of dying earlier or later, but of dying well or ill. And dying well means escape from the danger of living ill.

Interestingly, a full study of Seneca's work shows that he does not invariably look on old age in purely negative terms, as a stage of life to be avoided. As with Greco-Roman society as a whole, he betrays an ambivalent attitude toward aging. What is clear, however, is that a moral argument favoring suicide in old age depends upon the crucial Stoic idea of quality-of-life as the determinant of moral worth.

Yet this Stoic quality-of-life argument is open to certain objections. The most fatal objection is that suicide on grounds of old age contradicts the genuine first principle of Stoic ethics, the assumption that virtue alone is the only good and that virtue is happiness. Taken seriously, this principle requires us to say that quality-of-life is never determined absolutely by external gains or losses but depends on a radical freedom of the mind to take up new attitudes toward life circumstances. The Stoics always insisted that only the "things within our power" are our proper moral concern. Whatever fate may inflict by way of loss of fortune, bodily ills, and so on, the intrinsic freedom of the mind remains untouched.

What about the argument that the wise man should act before decline sets in, as when the Van Dusens chose suicide rather than face the prospect of debilitating old age? Isn't this suicide a form of "death-with-dignity" in contrast to the humiliating or dehumanizing fate symbolized by "dying in a nursing home," as the Van Dusens put it? As Paul Ramsey (1978) has argued we must view arguments for "death-with-dignity" with great care and skepticism. Must nursing home care inevitably be dehumanizing? Is not the humiliation feared really tantamount to a fear of dishonor, as the ancient Romans would have put it?

We know that death by suicide was common enough in ancient Rome. Brutus, Mark Antony, and Cleopatra, not to mention Seneca himself, are only a few from the long list of suicides on grounds of honor that were frequent in antiquity. In principle, this suicide to preserve dignity or avoid dishonor has much in common with *suttee*, the Hindu self-immolation of widows, or the Japanese *hari-kari*. We should perhaps look on all these claims to "dignity," "honor," or "ego-integrity" with some critical doubt. We need not approve of such self-killing when it is supported solely by a conception of the ideal self, too often reinforced by cultural norms that make life not worth living once a certain social role can no longer be maintained. Suicide because of fear of nursing homes or forced retirement should rather cause us to question those social practices that drive old people to kill themselves.

Both the balance-sheet argument and the quality-of-life argument for suicide on grounds of old age must be questioned through their most fundamental premises. Both the concept of "happiness" and "quality" presume a fixed or determinate picture of the self: only a certain sort of self, or a certain sort of life circumstance (e.g., Dr. Van Dusen's capacity to continue giving lectures) counts to make life worth living. Below some arbitrary level of happiness, or quality, life in old age does not measure up and so must be terminated.

Arguments favoring suicide in old age come down to the proposition that life in old age is no longer worth living. What happens all too often, if not inevitably, in old age is that sources of subjective meaning—reasons that made life worthwhile—one by one disappear. Through retirement from work roles, through the death of friends and loved ones, through the completion of life projects or the final failure of their realization— one by one the dreams and human purposes that made life worth living vanish. In this atmosphere, the real solution to the problem of suicide in old age is to find new purposes and new goals that make life worth living. This possibility, at bottom, is what we must understand to be Kant's insistence that man, as an end in himself, possesses the capacity to posit new goals, new ends for his existence, even in extreme old age, even until the last breath of life. This lofty standard is the meaning of human freedom and Kant's understanding of the moral law.

Conclusion

We live in a time when there are rising calls for the "right to die" and the need for "death with dignity." Today, ever larger numbers of persons are living to an advanced age where they are no longer economically productive and where they may become incapable of leading full and active lives. Under these circumstances, it becomes easy to describe the lives of the disabled elderly— those who are not terminally ill— as "meaningless." In this climate of opinion it is not difficult to foresee an extension of the growing tolerance for euthanasia to include a tolerance for suicide by those elderly whose lives have now been labelled "meaningless," by themselves or by others. In *Freedom to Die: Moral and Legal Aspects of Euthanasia*, Russell (1977) concludes:

It seems certain that it is only a matter of time until laws will be passed that will permit the administration of painless death when the only alternative is an agonizing or meaningless existence (p. 283).

We are embarked here on a very slippery slope indeed. In the case of suicide on grounds of age, the tendency is dangerous *not* because of any remote possibility of Nazi-like laws for obligatory euthanasia for the elderly. (*Newsweek*, May 12, 1969). Opponents of euthanasia who raise the Nazi spectre overlook the legal safeguards that make its adoption unlikely. No, the danger is not legally enforced euthanasia for the elderly but rather the spread of a climate of opinion that treats suicide among the elderly as a matter of libertarian indifference or as a welcome refuge from their problems. It is not difficult to imagine that in such a climate of opinion the unproductive, chronically-ill elderly would come to look on suicide as a ready alternative: they might even see avoidance of suicide as a matter of shame or cowardice —selfishly being a "burden on society." What was once a matter of disgrace would then become morally obligatory, even where not enforced by legal or institutional sanctions. When this happens, as Veatch observes, "natural death" will become, not merely a right but a duty.

If this possibility for such a radical reversal in moral attitudes seems remote, consider the way attitudes toward virginity and premarital sex have changed within a single generation. But we are not condemned to pure speculation in thinking about this subject, since historical precedents exist. The genuine historical precedent is not found in the Nazi case but among the ancient Romans, where suicide became common and acceptable, with philosophical support from the Stoic thinkers. The same Stoic arguments in terms of the "quality of life" of the elderly are increasingly being heard today. If life is "meaningless," then the logic of "administering" a painless death seems inevitable. But do we really want a society in which our best answer to the "meaningless" existence of old age is an encouragement for old people to kill themselves? Does this attitude itself not betray a contempt for dependence, a feeling that the lives of old people are somehow less than human, and, finally, a secret despair over the last stage of the life cycle?

On this point, I can do no better here than coincide with words from Erik Erikson that make clear just why the stakes seem to me so large in the question of suicide in old age. When we come to the last stage of the life cycle, writes Erikson (1964)

> . . .we become aware of the fact that our civilization really does not harbor a concept of the whole of life. . . . As our world-image is a one-way street to never ending progress interrupted only by small and big catastrophes, our lives are to be one-way streets to success—and sudden oblivion. Yet, if we speak of a cycle of life we really mean two cycles in one: the cycle of one generation concluding itself in the next, and the cycle of an individual life coming to a conclusion . . . . Any span of the cycle lived without vigorous meaning, at the beginning, in the middle, or at the end, endangers the sense of life and the meaning of death in all 'whose life stages are intertwined (pp. 132-133).

To live the span of old age in fullness of vigorous meaning requires, in Erikson's terms, the psychological virtue of *ego-integrity:* a strength and wholeness capable of withstanding the logic of suicide and its promise of a one-way sudden oblivion. But what we must understand is that the suicidal image of old age as despair is built into our current cultural crisis; it is a philosophical and ethical dilemma as much as anything else.

Eighty years ago William James wrote his book with the famous title, *"Is Life Worth Living?"* James certainly was a man well acquainted with despair, but as a physician and psychologist he saw quite clearly that the despair of suicide could only be overcome by answers that philosophical and religious thought would have to provide. Gerontology and thanatology alike need to look further in this direction to find new sources of meaning in the last stage of the life cycle. If our culture is to find an answer to this perhaps ultimate question of life, then those who study the phenomena of aging and death will·need to address the question that all of us must one day face.

REFERENCES

Choron, J. *Suicide.* New York: Charles Scribner's Sons, 1972.
Dworkin, R. *Taking Rights Seriously.* Cambridge: Harvard University Press, 1977.

Erikson, E. Human strength and the cycle of generations. In *Insight and Responsibility*. New York: W.W. Norton, 1964.

Euthanasia at 80? in *Newsweek*, May 12, 1969.

Fischer, J. Easy chair. In *Harper's Magazine*, February, 1973.

Gray, J. *Mill on Liberty: A Defence*. London: Routledge & Kegan Paul, 1983.

Kant, I. *Groundwork of the Metaphysics of Morals*. New York: Harper & Row, 1964.

Mill, J.S. On liberty. In *The Utilitarians: Jeremy Bentham and J.S. Mill*. New York: Doubleday, 1961, pp. 531-551.

Paton, H. J. *The Categorical Imperative: A Study in Kant's Moral Philosophy*. London: Hutchinson, 1958.

Portwood, D. *Common-Sense Suicide: The Final Right*. New York: Dodd, Mead & Co., 1978.

Ramsey, P. *Ethics at the Edges of Life*. New Haven: Yale University Press, 1978.

Russell, O. R. *Freedom to Die: Moral and Legal Aspects of Euthanasia* (Revised Edition). New York: Human Sciences Press, 1977.

The Van Dusen Case. *New York Times*, February 26, 1975, pp. 1, 43.

Chapter 8

RELIGION IN THE LIVES
OF THE ELDERLY
Contemporary and Historical Perspectives

W. Andrew Achenbaum

At the outset we are struck by one great partition which
divides the religious field. On the one side of it lies institutional, on the other personal religion. . . .Worship and
sacrifice, procedures for working on the dispositions of the
diety, theology and ceremony and ecclesiastical organization, are the essentials of religion in the institutional branch.
. . .In the more personal branch of religion it is on the contrary the inner dispositions of man himself which from the
centre of interest, his conscience, his deserts, his
helplessness, his incompleteness. '. . .The relation goes
directly from heart to heart, from soul to soul, between man
and his maker.

—William James (1901)

In this passage from *The Varieties of Religious Experience,* William
James formulated an insightful definition of "religion" and a sensible
way of approaching the subject matter. Most contemporary
theologians, religious scholars, and sociologists of religion would wish
to challenge, expand, modify, or at least qualify parts of James' state-

ment. Still, it does have virtues: his definition is brilliantly conceived, broadly focused and concisely written. For our present purposes, moreover, James' distinction between the personal and institutional components of religion is sufficient and instructive. Using his framework, I intend to review current research on the relationship between religion and the lives of the elderly. I shall also indicate aspects of that relationship which have shifted in importance and changed in meaning or function during the American experience. Finally, on the basis of this socio-historical analysis, I would like to offer some broad observations about the future and recommendations for future action.

I. "NEARER MY GOD TO THEE": RELIGION AND THE LIFE COURSE

I initially am concerned with understanding how individuals' intellectual, emotional, and spiritual responses to the realization and validation of who we are and where we are going are shaped by religious orientations. These are basic issues cutting to the core of the human condition. They become "religious" issues, I would argue, insofar as they are articulated, felt, and believed through an internalized system of conceptions and symbols, which are derived from "powerful, pervasive and long-standing" efforts to comprehend the relationship between "man and his maker."[2] My focus here is on individual responses, not collective beliefs and eschatologies or group behavior. Even more precisely, I limit my attention to ways that an individual makes sense of the general—indeed, transcendent—order of existence, assesses his or her place in it, and confronts the ultimate questions of life.

Three assumptions inform my discussion in this section. First, I do not think that there has been a significant psychosomatic or physiological change in the ways Americans "know" God. Ideas and feelings about God, religion, and faith are fluid and dynamic: they reflect and result from the impact of large-scale social, cultural, political, economic, and intellectual forces on our lives and the evolution of our society. But the cognitive process itself has not changed for centuries.[3] Second, like William James, I presume that there are varieties of religious experiences. Searching for an "ideal type" confounds more issues than it clarifies. Different religious viewpoints (including agnosticism and atheism) and modes of expression have long existed. Complexity in this area is thus not the exclusive hallmark of the current era. Third, while I am keenly aware of fundamental shifts in American religious beliefs and practices over time, I do not believe that these necessarily constitute a long-term trend toward "secularization," if by that term is meant the ultimate demise of organized religion or the growing irrelevance of religious teachings for individuals. The sacred and the secular have shaped American society, not just its religious dimensions, since the first settlement.[4] To be sure, the strands have become more differentiated and the interplay more diverse. But religion remains a critical force in America today.

Religious concerns, in fact, are quite prominent in late life. A 1958 Bureau of the Census survey indicated that less than 3 percent of all respondents over sixty-five reported having no religious preferences. This figure was somewhat smaller than the statistic for the population as a whole.[5] Subsequent public opinion polls and scholarly research underscore an unwavering belief in the existence of God among the elderly as well as the salient and stable role that religion plays in forming an older person's self-image. The studies also reveal that an increased interest in religion frequently occurs in later years: courses on the Bible and theology, for instance, are popular among older students, especially those new to adult education programs. There is ample historical precedent for this phenomenon. Religious concern among the aged is age-old. Early American church records, travel accounts, diaries, periodicals, poems, and graphics all present a consistent and vivid portrait of the breadth and depth of piety in old age: images of the venerable patriarch reading Scripture to his children and the old woman walking the path of righteousness to church are commonplace.[6]

Although the existence and persistence of religious concern in later life seems undeniable, the question of how religion affects life satisfaction in old age is quite problematic. Research during the past decade indicates a positive correlation between one's psychological well-being and religious involvement. It is not yet at all clear, however, whether adjustment in old age causes voluntary participation, or vice versa, or both. And even if we were to consider it highly

probable that deep faith contributes to a sense of balance and contentment past the age of sixty, we must be careful not to generalize too
hastily from this supposition. Religious commitments do not invariably assuage the emotional and mental strains occasioned by fear,
boredom, poverty, poor health, or isolation. The elderly's attitudes
about their imminent prospects suggest the difficulties in adjusting to
old age.[8] Nearly three decades of research on the subjective well-
being of older Americans confirm the fundamental importance of
health, followed by socioeconomic factors. Social interaction also is
conclusively related to life satisfaction, morale and contentment in
elderly subjects, though it is imperative to point out that the *type* of
social interaction is rarely specified.[9] Presumably, any meaningful interpersonal activity suffices. One is struck, in fact, by the surprisingly
few references to religious involvement in life-satisfaction research
models. (This may reflect a bias among gerontological researchers
and educators that is unwittingly reinforced by the federal government's reluctance to fund projects dealing with religious concerns and
themes.[10]) Far more research, which deliberately introduces and
operationalizes the issue of religion, must be done before we will
understand how, and under what circumstances, as well as to what
extent religious attitudes foster and strengthen a sense of well-being
in old age.

   We also need to explore more systematically the ways in which
elderly men and women apply their religious perspectives in assessing
the successes and failures of their lives. Nonetheless, it is possible at
this point to draw an analog between religion and life-review and to
see how they probably converge in old age. Considerable historical
evidence already exists indicating that religion provided an intellectual, emotional, and social milieu in which to understand how and
why grief developed the soul. To early Americans steeped in Protestant theology, "the Gospel has opened purer sources of consolation
than are to be found in Polytheism and heathen philosophy.[11] In this
context it was thought that the old helped to demonstrate the efficacy
of the advice set forth in consolatory literature. (Whether most aged
persons actually did adopt "correct" responses to tragedies is not
known). It is revealing, for instance, that John Adams (1816), an
astute observer of human nature, wrote in his ninth decade about the
need to face tragedy as a stoic Christian:

> Did you ever see a portrait, or a statue of a great man,
> without perceiving strong traits of pain and anxiety? . . .And
> who were these sad men? They were aged men, who had
> been tossed and buffeted in the vicissitudes of life—forced
> upon profound reflection by grief and disappointment—and
> taught to command their passions and prejudices . . .Grief
> drives men into habits of serious reflection, sharpens the
> understanding, and softens the heart; it compels them to
> arouse their reason, to assert its empire over their passions,
> propensities and prejudices; to elevate them to a superiority
> over all human events; to give them the *felicis animi immota
> tranquilitatum;* in short, to make them stoics and Christians. . .[12]

The means by which John Adams dealt with grief in his own "sad"
last years—reflection, self-control, resignation, tranquillity—have a
strikingly familiar ring.

Adam's recommendation sounds very much like the choice between "ego integrity" and "despair," which characterizes the last
stage of Erik Erikson's developmental theory of personality. Like
Adams, Erikson (1963) views the challenge of old age to be the
ultimate plateau in human development, one that builds on and syn-
thesizes previous life crises and decisions. Both men's perspectives,
moreover, are consonant with William James's assertion that "the
pivot round which religious life. . .revolves, is the interest of the individual in his private, personal destiny. Religion, in short, is a
monumental chapter in the history of human egotism.[13] A religious
commitment entails and facilitates a continuous assessment of one's
life in a way that does not impel doubt and cynicism, for a lively faith
simultaneously requires one to review past mistakes and wrongdoings
and to look forward. This is not always a happy enterprise: fear of the
"wrath of God," as Butler (1963) reminds us, often culminates in a
painful life review.[14] Nevertheless, it should now be clear why the
elderly, more than any other age group, potentially are best suited to
fathom the multiplicity and depth of symbolic meaning embodied in
religious forms, and why this creative gift, in turn, enables them to
reach higher levels of self-awareness than they previously achieved.
"Plenitude, finality, time, and meanings: these are the central or ax-
ial elements, the magnetic lines around which all the fragmentary bits
of aging and human experience organize themselves.[15] Religion has

provided, and continues to offer, vital directions and support for an older person putting life into perspective.

One can extend this line of reasoning a bit further and see the connections between aging, religion, and death. Once again there is much to learn from the historical record. Prior to the Civil War, philosopher, essayists, poets, and theologians contended that the wisdom and experience elderly Americans had accumulated through a lifetime of pleasure and pain taught them how to live and suffer properly. Having seen and survived all there was to experience on earth, the old were now in a position to perceive that which lay beyond. Such a vantage point, writers claimed, enabled older people to prepare to die in dignity. This theme received its most popular graphic representation in a series of allegorical paintings composed by Thomas R. Cole, a founder of the Hudson River School. Cole's conception of *Old Age,* the fourth picture in his *Voyage of Life,* reveals an ancient mariner (who was initially depicted as a babe sailing in a bright boat amid dazzling scenery) steering his battered vessel through a foreboding, rocky, barren landscape. Only a stream of light and host of angels dispell the gloom. As the artist describes the moment,

> The chains of corporeal existence are falling away, and already the mind has glimpses of Immortal life. The angelic being of whose presence until now the voyager has been unconscious, is revealed to him, and with a countenance beaming with joy, shows to his wondering gaze such as the eye of mortal man has never yet seen.[16]

According to the Romantic sensibility, the progressive course of personal, moral, and mental improvement reached its noblest elevation when one faces God and accepts the meaning of death in old age with equanimity and peace.

It is tempting to emphasize the parallels between the themes in Cole's painting and Erikson's assertion that achieving integrity in old age means facing death without fear. Such a stance, however, may exaggerate the degree of continuity in broad attitudes toward death and dying over time. It certainly underestimates the extent of change.[17] Death, after all, has become more age-specific in this country since the early 1800s. Then, death struck all age groups: infant and child mortality rates were very high. Now, thanks among other things to advances in medical technology and etiologies, improvements in diet and hygiene as well as better health care and environmental standards, life expectancy at birth has soared. While many still die "before their prime" from disease, epidemics, accidents, drug abuse, coronaries, and cancer, we view these deaths as "premature." Modernization has increased the odds that *we* will die in old age. Most "modern" Americans thus struggle to avoid death: we often displace our fear of it onto the elderly.

The aged themselves, studies consistently reveal, seldom express serious fears about death. Contrary to what we might expect, age is a poor predictor of who might be most suspectible to heightened fears and anxiety; severe disability and failing health do not invariably presage dread and fright. Fear of dying is most prevalent among the physically and socially isolated and the chronically depressed. Consequently, it has proved difficult for researchers to identify the independent, ameliorative effect religion might have on an older person facing his or her demise.[18] Devout believers and confirmed atheists evince fewer death fears than the sporadically religious. Religious conservatives seem more serene about dying than those who think they deserve retribution for their sins. But, once again, the data preclude definitive generalizations about the distinctive function of religion in preparing for natural death. Nor do we yet have a clear sense of religious positions on geriatric suicide or euthanasia in old age.[19] These are not new issues, of course, but recent transvaluations in ethical and cultural norms, not to mention the startling gains in our ability to control, program, and determine—clinically and legally—the precise moment of death, make such dilemmas controversial in novel ways.

In sum, this brief overview clearly demonstrates that personal religion is deeply entwined into a person's outlook and disposition in the last stages of life. Religion helps many older persons come to grips with the meaning of their lives as they wrestle with its finitude. Yet, if it is true that religion is an integral part of nearly everyone's life in later years, it is also evident that religious concern is neither invariably nor uniformly efficacious. More precise conclusions on this issue await more sophisticated analyses. Let us turn, then, to the elderly's involvement with religious organizations.

II. "A Mighty Fortress is our God":
The Aged and Institutional Religion

Just as William James underscored the varieties of religious experience, so too we must recognize the diversity of religious institutions in contemporary America. Fluid pluralism is a fundamental fact of religious life.[20] We are a nation of denominations, sects, and movements. These institutions differ remarkably in creeds, stance, liturgies, hierarchy, size, and commitment. Membership in a particular group tends to reflect one's ethnic and racial background. Within any mainstream Protestant denomination, Catholic diocese, or Jewish community, income and class play a part in determining which congregation one joins. But the point should not be overstated: given the freedom of choice and range of acceptable and available options, people frequently join a religious body that would have upset or appalled their parents. People also change congregations over the life cycle because of marriage and children, new friends, changing circumstances, and new emotional, spiritual, and intellectual needs and preferences. Because most people relate to their spiritual leader and interact with a specific set of members, every nationwide organization ultimately depends on its grassroots vitality. Parish life ebbs and flows.

Such localistic pluralism has been a perennial feature of American religious history. To be sure, middle-aged, white, English-speaking Protestants quickly established the tenor and set the pace of life in colonial America. But is it worth recalling that not all Protestants are alike, especially during a period of tremendous religious upheaval in Europe.[21] From the start, America was settled by factious groups—mainly Puritans, Anglicans, Quakers, Baptists, and Presbyterians—with wildly divergent beliefs. Others came. Roman Catholics dominated Maryland's political and social leadership; some Jews migrated and prospered in cities such as Newport, New York, Charleston, and Philadelphia. In the late seventeenth century, waves of German sectarians and French dissidents arrived, quickly establishing power bases in the Appalachian valleys. The spiritual beliefs of Indians and slaves were affected, but not adulterated, by contact with whites. Thus, even before the Revolution, religious toleration and prejudice prevailed in the new land. Overwhelmed by such diversity, it might be hard to imagine any unifying themes and interests that might have existed. Actually, there were many. In this section, I would like to discuss three that directly involve(d) the elderly.

One pattern common to nearly all early American religious institutions was the prominent role played by older members in local congregations. Unless a religious controversy or personal scandal caused divisions, ministers typically aged with their community, serving their congregations until death. The leading members of the laity tended to be older, though their standing was also a function of wealth, power, household size, and respect within the area. Some sects—such as the Shakers—literally chose their most senior brethren to serve as "elders," partly in keeping with their founders' teachings and partly to ensure fidelity with the original principles of the fold. Even those elderly members who did not serve in any official capacity made a visible contribution to communal life. Like the aged in many other preindustrial cultures, they maintained a ritual strength, corroborated by their accumulated wisdom, their proximity to departed ancestors, and their power to bless and curse.[22] Thus despite declining strength and diminishing fortunes, the aged's position in the church grew.

Older people do not figure as prominently in organized religion today. (Here, too, though, the data are incomplete and subject to several interpretations.) Most spiritual leaders retire at a prescribed time and manner as do other professionals. Priests, ministers, and rabbis are eligible for Social Security if they have made prior contributions. Most congregations make some provisions for their retired clergy; major denominations usually have a pension fund. Statistics on church attendance in old age vary greatly; no single statistic neatly applies across the spectrum.[23] Women are more likely than men to be involved in religious affairs. Blacks (particularly in low-income churches) and orthodox Jews generally maintain higher participation rates than other groups within the elderly population. Educational and regional differentials also have been uncovered. But I do not mean to imply that there is a precipitous drop in public worship in late life. On the contrary, it is essential to note an overall rise in church attendance over the life cycle, beginning in the late twenties. Regular worship patterns then persist through the seventh decade, when a slight decline does take place.[24] This probably reflects the difficulties associated with chronic illness, poor health, or transportation problems. Researchers have found that older people under these circumstances are likely to watch or listen to religious programs on television or radio. Church-related groups nonetheless constitute the voluntary association most frequently utilized by men and women over fifty-five; more than 50 of both sexes over seventy-five belong to a religious fellowship, if they participate in any group at all.

Yet, even though the elderly remain quite interested in maintaining their formal connections with their congregations, organized religion continues to be quite slow in responding to the needs of its older members. "While it appears that most churches are willing to *passively accept* the participation of older people in church affairs," observes Atchley,[25] "few are willing or able to *actively solicit* the participation of ill, handicapped, or isolated older people" (pp. 335-336). This posture hardly results from a dearth of ideas. For over 30 years, gerontologists and leaders within certain denominations have been recommending grassroots outreach services and housing programs for older people, age-specific educational and recreational activities within religious facilities, special training for clerical and lay leaders who minister to the old as well as greater cooperation and coordination with secular agencies. Some progress has been made. People in most communities know of at least one congregation that has established special programs for the elderly and hired qualified staff to assist in identifying and addressing older members' needs. The National Interfaith Coalition on Aging (NICA), which helps to direct activities among nearly three dozen denominations and agencies committed to promoting spiritual well-being among the aged, has been successful thus far in formulating and implementing fresh alternatives. But far more needs to be done.

This is not to suggest, of course, that organized religion has been insensitive to the woes associated with growing older. One of the most obvious manifestations of the Old Testament injunction "to honor thy mother and thy father" has been the significant contributions made in the social welfare area. Historically, officials in a community's largest and wealthiest Protestant congregations usually also served on the boards of public and private agencies that gave relief to the indigent old. Struggling antebellum Catholic parishes unstintingly allocated precious resources to help care for aging Irish and German immigrants, who often felt unwelcome or discriminated against in Protestant-dominated almshouses. Jewish congregations, in keeping with their deeply felt tradition of helping the old, provided tremendous support. Institutions catering exclusively to older members of particular denominations or nationalities were established, and upon opening, began to plan for expansion. Nearly two-thirds of the 1,200 benevolent homes operating in 1929 were founded between 1875 and 1919.[26] Many of these homes continue to flourish, though the denominational affiliation of prospective residents rarely is a criterion for admission or rejection. Thus one rarely finds a religiously homogeneous church home. Scandalous exceptions notwithstanding, most religious-based and operated homes are well managed, imaginative in programming, and provide quality care that goes beyond simply meeting basic physical needs.

There is a third link between organized religion and older Americans that merits scrutiny. It is more difficult to analyze than either the aged's participation in congregational life or the social welfare function of religious groups, because few church leaders, scholars, (senior) citizens, or public officials talk nowadays about the vital roles that older men and women once played in transmitting the ideals of America's revolutionary civic religion from one generation to the next.

As every civics text relates, our Founding Fathers deliberately separated the realms of church and state in the First Amendment to the Constitution. This dramatic step was taken because the people demanded it. The dangers of an established religion seemed painfully obvious in Britain's mistreatment of her colonies; there also was evidence that quasi-established denominations in the North and South abused their power. Freedom of religion thus had to be ensured along with all other civil liberties won on the battlefield and in legislative assemblies. The First Amendment, however, did not mandate that religious groups be apolitical or that governmental deliberations eschew moral underpinnings. Nor was this a popular idea during the formative decades of the Republic. Quite the contrary. Most Americans believed that Judeo-Christian precepts, particularly those espoused by evangelical Protestant churches ideally complemented the liberal-democratic-capitalist principles set forth in the Revolutionary era. A powerful civic religion thus pervaded antebellum American society and culture. Alexis de Tocqueville (1835), the brilliant

French student of political affairs and human relations, noted in his *Democracy in America*:[27]

> In France I had almost always seen the spirit of religion and the spirit of freedom pursuing courses diametrically opposed to each other; but in America I found that they were intimately united, and that they reigned in common over the country.
>
> Religion in America takes no direct part in the government of society, but nevertheless it must be regarded as the foremost of the political institutions of the country; for if it does not impart a taste for freedom, it facilitates the use of free institutions. Indeed, it is in this same point of view that the inhabitants of the United States themselves look upon religious belief. I do not know whether all the Americans have a sincere faith in their religion, for who can search the human heart? But I am certain that they hold it to be indispensable to the maintenance of republican institutions. This opinion is not peculiar to a class of citizens or to a party, but it belongs to the whole nation, and to every rank of society.

Devout older men and women, claimed writers at the time, embodied this civic religion. Those attaining old age, especially between 1790 and 1830, symbolically tied the present to the nation's revolutionary heritage.[28] By sharing the wisdom of experience and by offering guidance imbued with patriotic pride and religious rectitude, the elderly were immeasurably helping the young nation surmount its current dangers and lay a foundation for future growth.

Elements of that early civic religion still shape American life. With the exception of Washington's Second Inaugural Address (which was only two paragraphs long), every president has invoked the Diety as he set forth his vision for America upon taking office. Two decades after we went off the gold standard, we stamped *In God we trust* on our coinage. Patriotic holidays, such as Memorial Day, the Fourth of July and Thanksgiving, have large religious components. Still, it is clear that the tenor and impact of civic religion has changed over time. Influential scholars in the 1950s, such as Will

Herberg and Martin Marty (1959), asserted that American piety had grown flabby and become sentimentalized. Other students of religion, such as Robert Bellah, offered compelling arguments to justify civil religion in the 1960s, but there is a defensive quality to his remarks.[29] It now is fashionable for neo-conservatives to bemoan the lack of a profound sense of commitment that transcends our particular set of sociopolitical ethics and helps us to see our place in the universe.

This position receives its most cogent presentation in Daniel Bell's *The Cultural Contradictions of Capitalism* (1976). In previously published work, Bell had characterized the American experience during the second half of the twentieth century as ''post-industrial'' and argued that we have entered a new stage of societal development fraught with an unprecedented set of challenges and problems. But in this book, Bell[30] bemoans the excesses of the 1960s and urges a new cultural orientation.

> What I think the deeper currents of meaning are calling for is some new rite of incorporation, signifying membership in a community that has links with the past as well as the future. . . .To this extent, a religion of incorporation is a redemptive process whereby individuals seek to discharge their obligations that derive from the moral imperatives of their community: the debts incurred in being nurtured, the debts to the institutions that maintain moral awareness. Religion, then, necessarily involves the mutual redemption of fathers and sons. It involves the acknowledgement, in Yeats's phrase, of 'the blessed who can bless,' of the laying on of hands in the continuity of generations (pp. 170-171).

Bell's ''rite of incorporation'' is unabashedly conservative: he believes that civilization can only be preserved if young and old remain mindful and true to the privileges and responsibilities of the past and present.

I share Bell's opinion that revitalizing our civic religion is a legitimate and urgent priority, but I am not wholly persuaded by his thesis. I do not attribute our current malaise to ''the cultural contradictions of capitalism'' and hence do not search for an historically sensitive "post-modernist" ideology that will guide us deeper into the postindustrial order. Bell overstates his position, I think, by exaggerating the extent of historical disjunction in recent decades. On the one hand, it is not at all clear that we *have* entered a new phase of societal development. I would characterize the United States as an advanced industrial society. On the other hand, while I certainly agree that Americans' values systems have changed over time, I am nonetheless struck by the persistence of some of their central beliefs.[31] Hence "modernism" may well be a waning cultural force, but its obsolescence does not presage a radical shift in our world view. Furthermore, I suspect that I am more disturbed than Bell by the emerging coalition between the so-called "moral majority" and officials revamping social policies and reordering national priorities. Now, having distanced myself from some of the fallacious assumptions in Bell's critique, I would like to reformulate his prescription for future action.

Bell misleads us when he claims that the United States needs a "new rite of incorporation." We don't. Insofar as it goes beyond ephemeral, nationalistic goals and embodies the noblest universal and eternal aspirations of humankind, America's civic religion remains an appropriate standard by which to assess our success and failure as a people. What we need to do is to renew our pledge to the moral and political faith of our founding fathers and mothers in the early years of the Republic. This will require, among other things, that the rising generation rediscover the worth of older people as transmitters of a dynamic civic religion and that the aged themselves exercise greater leadership in helping all of us think through the moral ramifications of our public policies at home and abroad.

My chief recommendation for the future is that we take steps now to increase awareness of the distinctive religious needs of older people in order that we can better utilize the aged's current and potential contributions to American society. If my analysis is correct, then we can no longer afford to give religious issues a low priority in gerontological research and practice. Much more basic and applied research, along the lines I have suggested in this paper, must be conducted. Furthermore, clergy and other congregational leaders should take a more active interest in their aged members, involving them more fully in inter- as well as intra-generational activities. Improving the ministry to the old through all sorts of media deserves a high priority. For their part, the aged should be more forceful in articulating how and why their religious beliefs influence their thoughts and deeds. The elderly's oral histories, moreover, should do more than retrace individual memories; they should serve as a springboard for suggestions for future courses of action. Working with the young and the middle-aged, older Americans can help all of us see the connections between our personal destinies and our collective fate.

REFERENCE NOTES

1. James, W. *The varieties of religious experience* (originally published 1901-02); New York: Mentor Books, 1958. pp. 40-1. James only discussed "personal religion" in this volume, which was originally prepared as the Gifford Lectures to be delivered at the University of Edinburgh.
2. Here, I have amplified James's point by introducing a phrase from Clifford Geertz's *Religion as a cultural system,* quoted in Andrew M. Greeley, *The denominational society.* Glenview: Scott, Foresman & Co., 1972, 9.
3. James, J. *Origins of Consciousness and the Breakdown of the Bicameral Mind.* Boston: Houghton Mifflin Co., 1976, offers a brilliant development of this point.
4. See Lipset, S. M. *The first new nation,* New York: Basic Books, 1963, 168-9, and Parsons, T. Christianity and modern industrial society in Schneider, L. (Ed.) *Religion, Culture and Society,* New York: John Wiley & Sons Inc., 1964.
5. Moberg, D.C. Religiosity in Old Age. *The Gerontologist* June 1965, 5 pp. 78-87; Riley M.W. *et al. Aging and society* 3 vols. New York: Russell Sage Foundation, 1968-72, I:495. The link between religious concern and growing old is no longer considered self-evident, however. Compare the argument and tone of Paul B. Maves's Aging, Religion and the Church in Tibbitts, C. (Ed.) *Handbook of social gerontology.* Chicago: The University of Chicago Press, 1960, pp. 698-742, with the treatment of the topic by Atchley, R.C. *The social forces in later life.* (3rd ed.) Belmont, CA: Wadsworth Publishing Co., 1980, pp. 330-6;

and Hendricks, J. & Hendricks, D. *Aging in mass society*. Cambridge, MA: Winthrop Publishers, Inc., 1977, pp. 314-5.

6. Achenbaum, W.A. *Old age in the new land*. Baltimore: The Johns Hopkins University Press, 1978, Chapters 1-3; Fischer, D. H. *Growing old in America*. New York: Oxford University Press, 1977. Chapters 1-2; Douglas, A. *The feminization of American culture* New York: Knopf, 1977 pp. 196-9; Achenbaum, W.A. and Kusnerz, P.A. *Images of old age in America* Ann Arbor: Institute of Gerontology, 1978, Part 1.

7. Moberg, Regligiosity in old age. Riley *et al. Aging and Society*, I:496; Cutler, S.J. Membership in different types of voluntary associations and psychological well-being. *The Gerontologist* August 1976 *16*: pp. 335-9; Blazer, D. & Palmore, E. Religion and aging in a longitudinal panel. *Gerontologist* Feb. 1976 *16*: pp. 82-5.

8. Harris, C.S. *Fact Book on Aging* (Washington, D.C.: The National Council on the Aging, 1978), 148-151.

9. Larson, R. Thirty years of research on the subjective well-being of older Americans. *Journal of Gerontology* Jan. 1978 *33*: pp. 109-30; Hoyt, D. *et al.*, Life satisfaction and activity theory. *ibid*. Nov. 1980 *35*:pp. 935-42; Costa, P.A. *et al.*, Personal adjustment to aging. *ibid* Jan. 1981 *36:* pp. 78-86.

10. Atchley, R.C. *Social Forces,* p. 334. For the low priority accorded religion in gerontological core curricula, see Johnson, R. *et al.* Foundations for gerontological education, *Gerontologist* June 1980 *20*, Part 2; pp. 48, 50-1.

11. Review of the *Comforts of age,* in *Virginia Evangelical and Literary Magazine* June 1818 *1*; p. 271.

12. John Adams to Thomas Jefferson, 6 May 1816. In Bergh, A.E. (Ed.) *Writings of Thomas Jefferson* (20 vols.) Washington, D.C.: Thomas Jefferson Memorial Association, 1903-7, 15; pp. 14-5.

13. Erikson, E. *Childhood and society*. (2nd rev. ed.). New York: W. W. Norton, 1963. For a fuller statement, see Erikson's contribution to *Aging, death and the completion of being*, Van Tassel D.D. (Ed.) Philadelphia: University of Pennsylvania Press, 1979. The quotation comes from James's *Varieties*, p. 371.

14. Butler, R.N. The life review. *Psychiatry* Feb. 1963 *26*; pp. 65-76.
15. Moody, H.R. Aging and Cultural Policy. In *The arts, the humanities and older Americans,* Official Policy Symposium for the 1981 White House Conference on Aging. Washington, D.C.: National Council on the Aging, 1981, p. 11.
16. Mr. Cole's Pictures. *Knickerbocker* Dec. 1840 *16*, p. 54. For a fuller analysis of this point, see Achenbaum, *Old Age,* pp. 32-6 and 194, n. 26-7.
17. For an introduction to the history of death, see Aries, P. *Western attitudes toward death.* Baltimore: The Johns Hopkins University Press, 1976. and Stannard, D.E. (Ed.), *Death in America* Philadelphia: University of Pennsylvania Press, 1977. On the avoidance of death in modern thought, see Luckmann, T. *The Invisible Religion* New York: Macmillan Co., 1967, p. 114 and Becker, E. *The Denial of Death* New York: Free Press, 1973.
18. Jeffers, F.C. & Verwoerdt, A. How the old face death. In Busse W. E. and Pfeiffer E. (Eds.) *Behavior and Adaptation in Late Life,* Boston: Little, Brown & Co., 1969, pp. 163-81; Moberg, Religiosity. 505; Kastenbaum R. & Aisenberg, R. *The psychology of death* New York: Springer Publishing Company, 1972; Kalish, R. Death and dying in a social context. In Binstock, R.H. & Shanas, E. (Eds.) *Handbook of Aging and the Social Sciences,* New York: Van Nostrand Reinhold Co., 1976, pp. 483-510.
19. See, for instance, H.R. Moody in Chapter 7.
20. This summary builds on themes enunciated by Greeley, *Denominational Society,* 103-8. See also, W. Gerberg, *Protestant, Catholic and Jew,* (rev. ed.). New York: Doubleday & Co., 1955; Martin Marty, *The Righteous Empire.* New York: Dial Press, 1970.
21. Good introductions to this material include S.E. Mead, *The Lively Experience.* New York: Harper & Row, 1963; W. S. Hudson, *Religion in America.* New York: Charles Scribner's Sons, 1965; and S.E. Ahlstrom, *A Religious history of the American people.* New Haven: Yale University Press, 1972.

22. On this last point, see J. Goody, Aging in nonindustrial societies. In *Handbook of Aging and the Social Sciences*, 128; J. Demos, Old age in early New England. *American Journal of Sociology* November 1978, *84*, 6280-1; D. Guttmann, The cross-cultural perspective. In *Handbook of the Psychology of Aging*, J. E. Birren & K.W. Schaie (Eds.) New York, Van Nostrand Reinhold, 1977, 315-7.

23. Lowenthal M.F. & Robinson, B. Social networks and isolation. In *Handbook of Aging and the Social Sciences*, 445; Moberg, Religiosity, 501-3; Maves, Aging, religion & the church, pp. 736-7, 748; Atchley, *Social Forces*, 332; Hendricks & Hendricks, *Aging in Mass Society*, 315; Wingrave, C.R. & Alston, J.P. Aging and church attendance. *The Gerontologist* August 1971, *11*, 356-8.

24. Lowenthal, & Robinson, Social Networks, *ibid.;* Cutler, S.J. Age profiles of membership in sixteen types of voluntary associations. *Journal of Gerontology* November 1976, *31* pp. 462-70.

25. Atchley, *Social Forces,* pp. 335-6 See also the data and citations in Maves, Aging, religion and the church, pp. 720-3.

26. U.S., Bureau of Labor Statistics, *Care of Aged Persons in the United States,* Bulletin no. 489 (Washington, D.C.: Government Printing Office, 1929), pp. 131, 176, 193. See also G.B. Nash, Poverty and poor relief in Pre-Revolutionary Philadelphia. In *Colonial America*. Katz, S.N. (Ed.) Boston: Little, Brown, 1976, pp. 375-401; M. Zimmerman, Old-age poverty in preindustrial New York City. In Hess, B. (Ed.) *Growing Old in America*, New York: Transactions Press, 1976, p. 88.

27. de Tocqueville, A. quoted in Ahlstrom, *A religious history*, 386. See also J. Higham, Hanging together. *Journal of American History* June 1974, *61*, pp. 16-18; Gabriel, R.H. Evangelical religion and popular romanticism in early nineteenth-century America. *Church History* March 1950, *19*, p. 45.

28. Achenbaum, *Old age*, pp. 23-4; Middlekauff, R. The ritualization of the American revolution. In *The development of American culture*. S. Coben & L. Ratner (Eds.) Englewood Cliffs: Prentice-Hall, Inc. 1970, pp. 31-44.

29. Herberg, W. *Protestant, Catholic, Jew.* Marty, M.E. *The New Shape of American Religion* New York: Harper & Row, 1959, pp. 37-39; Bellah, R.N. Civil religion in America, *Daedalus* Winter 1967, *96*, pp.1-21; Greeley, *Denominational society,* Chapter 7.
30. Bell, D. *The cultural contradictions of capitalism.* New York: Basic Books, 1976.
31. For a fuller elaboration of my position, see the first chapter of my *"Modern" values and aging America.* Cambridge, MA: Winthrop Publishing Company, 1982.

Chapter 9

CARING FOR THE ELDERLY
Religious Institutions

Jerome Kaplan

The home for the aged in the United States has been a primary source of leadership and service to the elderly since the turn of the century. The nonprofit home, usually of religious concern and sometimes a fraternal one, set the tone for the service of the future.

The National Association of Jewish Homes for Aging held a significant conference in 1973. At this meeting alternatives to institutional care were discussed in rational terms. Parallel systems of care were noted. Comprehensive community involvement was stressed. But most important for the basic point to be made herein, it was noted that alternatives had been emerging for at least over 30 years; that the nonprofit home for the aged has been in the forefront of the outreach service; and that such homes already serve as cornerstones for the talked-about services of today but which in many instances were long demonstrated as viable through the institution-based approach.

Although not described herein, it should be mentioned—among other programs—that the longest continuous Meals-on-Wheels service in the U.S. with full, individual diets provided to an entire community is institutionally based and institutionally motivated; that independent housing, whether through apartments, cottages, or other modes was institutionally motivated and begun; that major home health aide services were initiated through the institution; that the physical, occupational, and speech therapies to the elderly for outpatient and in-house service was institutionally pushed, along with the then newer, added concept of the importance of such therapies for maintenance; and, at the time of this meeting, religious-based institutions had already begun adult daycare; were beginning the hospice experiment; and, the list can grow. In 1964, for example, *Geriatrics* carried an article on *An Analysis of Multiple Community Services Through the Institution for the Aged* by J. Kaplan. In 1966 the same author wrote on *Measuring the Impact of a Gerontological Counseling Service on a Medical Community* in the *Journal of Gerontology;* in 1967 *The Gerontologist* printed *Appraising the Traditional Organizational Basis of Providing Gerontological Services,* and, earlier in 1957, 20 years prior to the governmental movement, *Geriatrics* published *The Day Center and the Day Care Center.* The documentation is incontrovertible. Research undertaken through the Philadelphia Geriatric Center, the Dallas Golden Acres Home for Aged and Mansfield (Ohio) Memorial Homes—and others—has substantively contributed to our gerontological knowledge.[1]

AN HISTORICAL PERSPECTIVE

The story of the early days of this world and the creatures who inhabited it, as set forth in the Old Testament, glosses over the everyday struggles that were necessary for people to keep alive. The family groups, the tribes, or the nations were depicted as self-protective, bellicose, even militant—everyone had to fight for sheer survival. But gradually the human being's development as a cooperative individual begins to take shape—responsiveness to purpose instead of an aimless struggle simply to survive—is discerned. This purpose is the ethical imperative, and the Old Testament stories relate how the moral way of life was made the ideal to be followed. The Cain-Abel legend was to teach the dire consequences of failure to control one's emotions. "Am I my brother's keeper?" was translated into an ethical taunt of conscience to which the only acceptable answer was an affirmative.

The positive approach is strongly supported in telling about the

Patriarch Abraham, credited with originating institutions such as hotels, hospitals, and homes by legends that tell of his tent at crossroads formed by the junction of important trade routes.[2] It had openings on four sides and was accessible from every direction. Strangers were welcomed, given to eat and drink, made comfortable for the night, and in the morning were set upon the road headed in the right direction.

"God loves the stranger"[3] served as inspiration to indicate the intensity of effort that was made to accommodate those who journeyed to Judea. It was the aspiration to develop a people extending a whole range of amenities, comforts, and necessities for those in the community who were deprived. Providing food, clothing, education for children, doweries for maidens, subsidies for orphans, visitors to the sick, support for pregnant women, money for free burials, ransom for captives, aid to the ailing, and shelter for the aged, were equated with the highest ideals of mankind.[1] Maimonides, a physician and philosopher in Judaism supported the concept that such aims were intended not only for the Jewish constituency but to be practiced on behalf of all people alike, undertaken voluntarily by each individual.

In Ecclesiastes and the Psalms there are references to the infirmities of the declining years, the failing powers of the aged. Old Age also was pointed to as a state of inactivity. To balance this, an obligation was placed upon the young to provide for the support and comfort of the old[5] and without question, the Commandment[6] indicating that honor should be given to one's father and mother is in a like vein.

Charity is more than giving help. Refining of the ideals, first bearing concern about "one's brother," that gradually enlarged to include the "poor," continued. The charitable deeds that were conferred upon the poor served as one's personal obligation to bestow kindness and to do justice under the principle of Zedaka. The collective understanding that the intended recipients were the rich and poor alike, so long as there was a request for assistance, began slowly but steadily to gain acceptance. The next step was to recognize that it was beyond the mere donating of money that was involved. The succeeding move was the elevation of the idea that consideration for the needs of the many in their manifold ramifications constituted a matter of public safety. In turn this called for entrusting sponsorship to public auspices, to take it out of the hands of the religious hierarchy.[7] A ladder of *Zedaka* (loosely translated as "Charity" but more appropriately "Justice") was developed by Maimonides, wherein each step increased the worthiness of a good action. The intent of Zedaka was for a recipient of benefactions to be spared a sense of shame and for a benefactor to so provide assistance as to help the recipient to help himself.

This compares with the concept of "liberalities" of the Roman world, where the freeborn (*libre*) demonstrated their generosity by making munificent donations in favor of the lower classes. It was the means toward building up the countless sums of money that poured into every avenue of service and succor considered needful in those times.

Not every individual was in a position to perform the obligations that were promulgated; thus answerability devolved mostly upon the rich. During the Middle Ages, however, more of the burden began to be assumed by benevolent societies formed for these purposes. This had the effect of removing individual givers and receivers from direct contact and thus helped to perfect the rationale for public agencies, opening the way toward institutionalization.

Varied Facilities for Various Care Types

In the Near East countries, homes of all kinds existed to care for Jewish convalescent, incurable, and aged persons. To facilitate the movements of Jewish travelers and merchants, way-stations for strangers were common in many villages. From the time of the first Crusade these were turned into hospitals. Actual records of some Jewish communities from about the eleventh century on tell about procedures established to dispense alms, arrange funerals, ransom oppressed peoples, lend money without interest, visit the sick, and house the aged. Many such homes for aged were located in France, maintained by local Jewish organizations. And in Germany, there were similar installations—*Pszundnerhauser*—32 in all. In almost every country on the continent there were at least a few institutions or organizations that customarily provided the various kinds of relief for which there was need.

Across the Channel in England, the Hebrew Philanthropic Society of Birmingham granted aged pensions, while the Hebrew

Provident Society did likewise in Liverpool and Manchester. The Jewish Board of Guardians and Relief Society in various parts of the British Empire, including Sydney, Australia, took care of the aged poor and sponsored homes for the aged.

In the Roman lands, in pre-Christian and early Christian centuries, there were hospices or public inns, called *Pandoks,* usually built on the high road, that offered shelter and food to the poor traveler.[8] To the Essenes, a defunct Jewish sect, is ascribed the origination of the eleventh century institutions that came to be known as *Xenodochia,* or inns for strangers. As part of the pattern, in various areas, these quasi-institutions were connected with or served also as *Ptochia,* or *Ptochotrophia,* that is, sick houses. There is evidence that the Emperor Julian, as a policy of his regime encouraged the setting up of Inns for Strangers in every city.[9] Seneca mentions *Valetudinaria* or infirmaries for slaves, that also were used by free Romans in the first century. At Beth Saida, from a mention in the New Testament, we learn of the existence of a *Bet Holim* or Jewish hospital that was situated in a wooden hut. In the excavations at Pompeii certain facilities were discovered indicating they were modern hospital-like conveniences for physicians. Persia and Arabia also had hospitals supported by kings and rulers before the Christian Era, and the Greeks had the Temple of Aesculapius at Epidaurus.

The term hospital seems to have served as a designation for a section of a dwelling or home that was set apart for the treatment of the sick. It is known that in early times isolation of certain contagious diseases, as leprosy, called for establishing a "house of separation"[10]; otherwise maladies were treated on the family's hearth and institutional placement was required only for ailing strangers.

Here and there in the civilized world, various health care facilities were established. India, in the third century, was known for its well disposed units called *latreria.* A fourth century Christian lady, Fabiola, established the first charity institution in Rome, and the spread of Christianity extended such establishments elsewhere in Italy and France at that same period, although it took centuries longer to achieve more adequate coverage in Europe. However, the Moslem world had extensive facilities by the year 800.

England in the eleventh and twelfth centuries had listings of 980 hospitals, but after the thirteenth century the number dropped. Siting hospitals was a delicate procedure. Usually they were located outside the walls of the towns and, if possible, on a river bank. This was a simplified form of isolation to counter the spread of disease. The size of those medieval hospitals usually counted up to 30 beds. Although it is difficult to establish a difference in function, there were also infirmaries that served some purpose connected with health care.

Whatever existed in the way of facilities to help people usually were in the hands of monks' Orders. The individual commitment did not hold for all persons, even those who could afford it, and even the conscience of the community was not always equal to the challenge. However, the sixteenth century English Reformation Parliament was anxious to break up the hold of the church and proceeded to wrest control of institutions engaged in communal services from clerical authority. It followed that by ordering the dissolution of the monasteries, all institutions under religious auspices, including existing hospitals, by this one blow, ceased to function. Nevertheless certain purposeful religious members'clandestinely contravened the new laws.

Matters came to a head in England early in the seventeenth century upon passage of the Poor Law Act. The new system of public relief instituted thereunder erected poor houses where society's castoffs were placed in custody of wardens and matrons.

Medicine as a science had begun to show some value for human beings, and the work in the hospitals was especially stimulating to the public interest. In fact physicians favored hospitals over the patient's home. Even as today, the physician found it a better milieu for teaching, for research, for treating more than one patient at a time; the patient was in a better environment, and it could be controlled. The best medical talent and minds set about arranging metes and bounds that had little regard for the economic status of the patient. Instead, admissions had to satisfy scientific requirements. In the screening, preference was shown the acutely ill. It was true then, as today, that campaigns for funds could not expect success in stressing care of the chronically ill, and those who sought training and study were impatient at and felt unrewarded in work with long-term patients. In fact, the beginning of the splintering into specialty areas found its start at that time and as a consequence hospitals became selective as to categories of disease treated—and, alas, the chronic patients and long-term sufferers were the elderly. With the kind of specialization that was being encountered, a void was felt in the community and, as reaction thereto, again the church stepped in, setting up a system of public relief administered by pastors of local churches.

Elderly Continue Receiving Marginal Attention

The public conscience in time became aware of injustices, but aged people were not the focus of political pressures. As a matter of fact, the goals were multi-pronged—more relief, more health care, more poor houses, and the like. But the aged constituted only a small segment of the bigger problem of relief for the poor, and though there was much activity, the aged tended to be bypassed. The new legislation continued to lump them indiscriminately with the "needy," diminishing their own significance to a minute percentage of the whole problem.

There were, however, signs that in certain sections agitation was being stirred up about the tendency to address conditions affecting the able-bodied poor, while conditions of the sick, handicapped, and aged that so desperately needed attention were overlooked. Sheltering persons who thus lived at public expense in institutions led to invoking a regulation that required work to be done by all men, exemplifying the Protestant ethic that everyone had to be gainfully engaged, except those declared to be too sick. The elderly once again found themselves caught in the middle. While not the direct target of the challenge, they became the butt of finger-pointing, highlighting the belief that an improvident old age was the result of a misspent or dissolute life.

U. S. History – Select Aspects

There are records of homes for aged in this country that were founded more than 140 years ago. Scattered throughout the United States, though their names may have even changed, the legal successors have continued, usually at the same location, to carry out the objectives in their charters. Most homes were established after the turn of the century. Usually religious denominations, immigrant aid societies, or the like stimulated the founding, or acted as primary organizers of such voluntary institutions.

In general it was set out that applicants had to comply with requirements respecting physical condition, age, property, and residence mandates, and in some instances were required to hold membership in the organization. Some homes accepted only men, others only women, although 60 percent admitted both sexes. Nearly one-half made no financial demands, while others required weekly or monthly charges or entrance fees, usually $500, but in some cases thousands. In some homes the residents were expected to "lend their services at small duties around the home."

One home that accepted only Presbyterian ministers who did not use tobacco in any form, had not had any applicants in many years and in fact soon closed its doors. One home, endowed by a rich man, was located "in landscaped grounds of a beautiful residential suburb," with living rooms the last word in comfort, even approaching luxury. At the other end were the homes that furnished the barest of necessities—plainest food, beds, and dormitories with 30 to 35 residents making privacy impossible and comforts very scarce. In such homes even "a split rocker was regarded a luxury," and the dormitories were kept locked during the day. There was a middle group where attempts were made at a real home, with matrons who sought to harmonize the tastes of from 10 to 200 people. The matrons prided themselves on the fact that "the inmates have nothing to do but enjoy themselves."

The first Catholic Home in the United States was the Lafon Asylum of the Holy Family established in 1842 in New Orleans, operated by the Sisters of the Holy Family, a black congregation. Another religious order, the Sisters of the Third Order of St. Francis, began caring for sick elderly in their own homes at about the same time in Buffalo, New York, and in 1855 they established the St. Francis Home in Buffalo. Religious groups and national immigrant associations also were involved in establishing homes for aged in those years. The Home for Aged and Infirm Israelites, the first known Jewish institution, was founded in St. Louis in 1855, and almost every national group of European origin and even particular sections of various countries established homes for aged, many of which continue at their old sites today.

A most prominent religious group involved with homes for aged is the Little Sisters of the Poor. This organization's first home in the United States was founded in Brooklyn in 1868. Later the same year other branches established homes in Cincinnati and New Orleans, and by 1874 there were 13 homes under their auspices.

Homes for the aged were started originally for the poor, but certain factors led to expanding on the concept of institutions for elderly men and women. Some had their own funds and entered homes upon payment of a lump sum for life care, to gain security for their remaining years. This arrangement cast up its own complement of problems, not the least of which was the realization that frequently payments for life care were not adequate. Not only did the patients live longer than expected, but criticism was encountered because planning and administration were not equal to surmounting other difficulties. In Catholic circles the diocesan authorities in some cases came to the rescue financially. In Erie, Pennsylvania, a home of the Sisters of St. Joseph was destroyed by fire, whereupon the bishop arranged for its replacement. A similar home in Syracuse built in 1921 had the help of the Catholic Church, and the diocese of Green Bay, Wisconsin, undertook financial responsibility in 1927 for a local home.

A Superior of the Little Sisters of the Poor, Mother Angelene Teresa, saw a need for homes for persons with some means. Her Order was limited to serving only the poor. In 1929 with six companions she founded the Carmelite Sisters for the Aged and Infirm. In 1930 the Catholic Church made a grant enabling the Carmelite Sisters to buy a building in the Bronx, New York, that became St. Patrick's Home for the Aged and Infirm. In 1910 there were 98 Catholic Homes; in 1930, 142; in 1946, 171; in 1958, 314; and in 1962, 355 with 34,000 residents.

TREATMENT RESOURCES AND THEIR APPLICATION

The treatment of aging has two general levels: the provision of treatment resources and the application of those resources. Even a third level might be distinguished: namely, the reception of assimilation of treatment resources on the part of those being treated.

Treatment Resources

The provision of treatment resources for the aged refers most obviously to the federal government, to public and private agencies and institutions, especially religious-based institutions, and to professional personnel. Not to be overlooked, of course, are families and the patients themselves. Ultimately, all taxpayers are involved on this level of treatment and in a particularly critical sense so too are the entire socioeconomic and sociophilosophical orders, both national and local which the mainstream of people participate in, embody and represent.

With respect to the application of treatment resources, at least four points of reference can be distinguished. First, there are the categorical groups for which respective treatment resources are intended and/or designed. Second, there are the categorized individuals within those groups. Third, there is the application of treatment resources by means of institutional methodologies, the hospital, the home for aged, the nursing home, the residence. Fourth, and perhaps of particular significance for the future, is the application of treatment resources via parallel methodologies, both structured—such as in the case with visiting nurses associations, personal care organizations, homemaker/health-aide services, meals-on-wheels and religious institutions with organized services—and the nonorganized, such as family, neighborhood, church, and civic initiatives.

Treatment Assimilation

On the level of treatment reception or assimilation, such measurable factors as personal need, individual and group psychology, patient involvement, and auxiliary supports have to be distinguished. Similarly, such intangibles as patient or client willingness, individual life-style, coping resources, spiritual well-being, the ebb and flow of relationships, and environmental influences must be attended.

Fortunately, not all the problems to be met within the treatment of aging are ethical problems. Some are merely technological, methodological, procedural, or logistical. Some, however, are essentially ethical in nature, entailing decision making that has direct, and, at times, irreversible repercussions on the well-being of persons. Others have only an ethical facet or dimension, dealing substantially with the manipulation of nonhuman entities but having implications or consequences for persons touched in some way by that manipulation.

Ethical Base

For present purposes, an ethical situation is one involving human decision, human repercussion, and an evaluation of both in terms of human well-being. According to Western tradition, an ethical act requires the measuring of human decisions and consequences against the essential expectations or requirements of human nature. To undertake to meet that measure, through the process of judgment called conscience, is to act ethically and well; it is to perform a good action. By derivation, it is to be a good person, at least in terms of what one has done. To decline that measurement, on the other hand, or to decide against its imperative, is to act unethically and badly. It is to perform an evil action, and, by derivation, to be an evil or bad person, at least in terms of what one has done or failed to do.

There never has been unanimity on the conceptual structure of human ethics. Even the core concept of the Western tradition has repeatedly been the subject of debate. It is challenged in part as it affects the aged, and clues as to the import of why some challenge is necessary have already been indicated.

To employ general, undifferentiated humanness as the measure of human interaction is certainly to indicate, if not demonstrate, the basic humaneness (or inhumaneness) of human actions. According to that measure, human decision making must always be humane. It must be in keeping with the dignity of both the person deciding and the person or persons decided about. Failing that measure, one faults both oneself and whoever is to experience the effects of that fault.

Moral Actions in Treatment

It is possible to establish an extensive catalogue of moral and immoral actions with respect to the treatment of the chronically ill and aged. Such actions as the following illustrate this:

1. Negotiation or imposition of treatment options
2. Provision of adequate or inadequate nutrition
3. Maintenance or disregard of patient privacy.
4. Promotion or restriction of unnecessary institutionalization.
5. Therapeutizing or dehumanizing treatment methodologies.

6. Processing or neglect of patient care, including the inability of a physician to visit a nursing home patient.
7. Servicing or exploitation of patient deficits.
8. Provision or disregard of safety and security measures.
9. Professionalizing or desensitizing treatment personnel.
10. Unifying or compartmentalizing related treatment resources.
11. Liberation or prolongation of patient dependencies.
12. Provision or withholding of related treatment supports or resources.

In our culture some of the more gross immoralities regarding mistreatment of the aged are also crimes, actions specifically prohibited by statute or legal precedent. In this respect public law is another repository of consent to the substance of the Western ethical tradition.

Any departure from the classical ethical norm should note two operative accompaniments. (1) As there are gross immoralities in the treatment of the chronically ill and aged, so there are also dramatic instances of morality, that is, instances of superlative correspondence with the norm of humaneness. (2) By no means are all instances encompassed by the catalogue of previously listed illustrations dramatically clear in their rightness or wrongness. There may well be situations and facets of situations inferred in that catalogue that defy clarification, whose resolution at best may lie only in a selection of the lesser evil, and at worst in an opaque and often heartrending, "damned if you do and damned if you don't" toss-up.

Moral Actions in Provision

The illustrations cited earlier deal mainly with the application level of treatment resources. Similar illustrations of moral and immoral actions can be noted on the provision level of treatment resources; for example:

1. Assurance of adequate or inadequate income suppports.
2. Provision or denial of feasible care options.
3. Provision or disregard of the social components of care.
4. Enacting or impeding of adequate protective laws.
5. Processing or neglect of cost control mechanisms.

6. Application or detouring of categorical care allocations.
7. Setting or inhibiting of relevant public priorities.
8. Renewal or endorsement of entrenched resource and treatment systems.
9. Correction or perpetuation of categorical myths.
10. Correction or perpetuation of entrenched vested interests.
11. Provision or prohibition of spiritual well-being resources.
12. Compensation or requirement of competitive inequalities.

It is here that a legislator's decision, for example, can have repercussion on millions of chronically ill and aged persons, and a subsequent presidential or gubernatorial decision can change it all. Prior to such decision, however, one must note the entire socio-psychological context that contributes to their evolvement. In a sense it relates to corporate responsibility, including merit and guilt, a concept reappearing of late in certain Christian theologies (Hartman, 1963).

On the provision level of treatment, then, one meets interlocked value systems, degrees of social consciousness and social conscience, overlays of previous ethical fallout, surges of ethical evolution, entrenched inhibitors of change and growth, and whatever other factors are operative in the process that gives a body politic its ethical identity. On this provision level, in a word, the gigantic problem of public policy formulation is met interfaced by our social policy evolvement, the matrix ethical problem involved in the treatment of the chronically ill and aged.

Classical Norm

To approach this problem, it is necessary to take issue in part with the basic ethical norm of the classical tradition. The problem at hand is too critical to be processed through the prism of general, undifferentiated humanness; the problem is one of very specialized humanness, requiring a measure of unique rather than general humaneness.

Morality is measured, according to Western norm, by the compatibility or discrepancy of human decisions with all the requirements that are essentially rooted in or related to human nature. An intellectually sophisticated construct, this norm provides the weights and measures of ethics for general human behavior on the part of the general run of persons.

The classical ethicists are not to be faulted for any failure to give due consideration to categorical and individual differences in general human nature. By an elaborate and multifaceted doctrine of circumstances, they interpreted general humanness as distributed through a multiplicity of categorical and individual variations, out of which were drawn the ethical implications. The weak of mind, for example the senile, were thus seen as accountable only in proportion to the strength and scope of their lucid moments.

Nor are the savants of ethics to be held responsible for what the beneficiaries of their legacy would do with it. How were they to perceive nuances of a democratic society, destined to arise long after their theorizing, whereby general nature is ascribed to the general run of people, to the majority, and restricted nature to minorities? Or, if that be too harsh, how were they to know that socially, politically, economically, militarily, educationally, and even religiously, general human nature would repeatedly support the claims of the established order, and with the same persistence urge the denial of the claims of subgroups?

What the classical ethicists bequeathed to us is an abstruse norm albeit a humanizing development beyond the ancient Greek hubris and the Roman paternalism. It is a great improvement also over the primitive revelation of the Hebrews, synopsized in caricature by the doctrines of "an eye for an eye" and the "doom" of national enemies. Further, it is a convincing alternative to the "Superman" pattern of Nietzsche and the Nazis and the organized racism of the Ku Klux Klan.

In spite of its credits, the classical norm suffers a variety of intrinsic and extrinsic deficiencies. For example, it has a tendency to support restricted social systems. With respect to that tendency, the fault in question may ultimately be more attributable to the moral weakness of its devotees and followers than to the deficits of the norm itself. If the historical odyssey of that norm, or of any moral norm for that matter, teaches us anything, it is that a schedule of moral goals or requirements, no matter how accurately drawn, is not of itself an effective instrumentality for its own achievement. If morality were solely science, would not then our generation and times be the most moral of all eras?

Morality requires, in addition to a clear schedule of goals, corresponding and harmonious behavior, decision making and follow-through compatible with those goals. It is at this point that human initiative chronically breaks down. A norm of moral truth and fidelity is perhaps not as attractive as the things that rival it and is less tangible. On the other hand, there is an attractiveness about truth and moral goodness that is not unfamiliar to the mainstream of men and women. My point is that the classical norm fails to exploit that attractiveness. This is its external deficiency.

As I read contemporary commentators on the classical norm, its originators had at their disposal only only an insight into the static and consummately constituted facets of human nature (Dupre, 1964).

Intuitions of differentiation, particularity, and change they certainly had, but nothing akin to the fuller view of humanness now available in synthesis of modern psychological, sociological, philosophical, and even biological insights (Curran, 1968). This is its intrinsic difficulty. Today, for example, the mainstream of thinkers, scientists, and practitioners are as comfortable with an evolutionary view of humanness as were the classical ethicists with their absolute view. The very mutuality of this comfort would suggest that a more adequate and operative view of humanness would involve a pairing of the two perspectives. Both, I believe, are true, as far as they go. Neither, however, is of much long-term help in isolation.

Change in the Classic Norm

Human nature is essentially developmental; with this construct, human nature is essentially aging. Further, chronic illness is a constitutive component of humanness, certainly as to its developmental implications, whether progressive or retrogressive, and perhaps also as to its very being. Maves (1965) has observed the following:

> I submit the hypothesis that the nature of religious experience may be different at different stages of adult life because of the way in which the Holy and the Unconditioned is customarily encountered. Therefore, the forms of religious expression will need to be different to take account not only of the experience itself but also of the changed capacities and

needs of the person. Thus, the institutionalized expressions of religious experience and faith need to be examined to see whether or not they are adequate to deal with the new length of years that medical science has added to us (pp. 69-79).

Implicit in what Maves perceived as the developmental roots of religious experience, expressions, and needs is the deeper perception, I believe, of the developmental roots of aged persons themselves. Such persons are versions of embodiments of processive human nature. As such, they represent not general, undifferentiated humanness, but specialized, and to a unique degree, actualized and finalized humanness. Furthermore, the norm of humanness demanded by their unique being is one not of general dignity and morality, such as the traditional norm established for all persons, but of uncommon and wholly specialized responsibility. If it be sound, as Maves suggested, that the institutionalized aspects of religion need to be re-examined in light of a developmental theory of religious experience, it seems even more sound that institutionalized treatment resources for the aged, on both the application and provision levels, demand re-examination if developmental theory is pertinent to humanness itself.

There is an attractiveness to the construct. Moreover, implications for responsibilities and actions are far more clearly directed and specific than disclosed by the classical moral norm. Ultimately, there are stronger grounds for a more insistently humane psychology and public policy regarding categorical groups than are to be found with the classical ethical norm.

Chronology alone, however, is not necessarily an operative measure of the humanizing process. We all know that comprehensive human development issues from a concurrence of a multiplicity of stratified vitalities, some normally following a chronological age and quite independent of absolute age correlation. We know, too, that developmental vitalities often fail to materialize or they materialize unequally or at least unevenly, thus spawning the whole gamut of personality and psychosocial variations among people.

Proposing an expanded and fuller humanness in the elderly, therefore, means the elderly are more fully human not solely for what has actually developed within them but also for their potential development. In some instances they are marked mainly by actualization: Some older persons are richly endowed with abilities, great in their social achievements, and noble in moral stature. In other instances they are marked mainly by potentiality. Usually, though, older persons are marked by a combination of both.

Whether aged or not, humanness touched congenitally, accidentally, or pathologically by chronic disability is a uniquely intensified humanity. Thwarted in normal channels of expression, at times even frustrated entirely, the vitalities of a chronically ill person must necessarily be regrouped, redirected, and compensated in an intensive, alternative way.

This construct of the aged is attractive. There is an objective dignity and order of entitlement here, perhaps both clearer and stronger than that offered us in the Western ethical tradition.

How, then, do we reconcile the thinking of one of the most lucid men who ever lived—the Roman stoic thinker Seneca—if he showed the desire to act upon the following thought in a modern society:

> Few have lasted through extreme old age to death without impairment, and many have lain inert. . . .I shall not abandon old age, if old age preserve me intact for myself. . .but if old age begins to shatter my mind, and to pull its various faculties to pieces, if it leaves me, not life but only the breath of life then I shall rush out of a house that is crumbling and tottering (Epistle LVIII).

Thus we see the continued challenge in caring for the elderly as a challenge to our religious institutions. Can an increased lifespan be achieved without keeping marginally functioning individuals alive for extended periods? Would a major increase in the proportion of the aged so aggravate the problems of health, medical care, income, and housing that the old would be worse off than now? What would be the major deleterious and the major beneficial effects of a prolonged lifespan upon the rest of society? Will free time be truly free—that is, will it be desired by most individuals? Can it be supported? Will it be socially honored? Will our social and humanistic and ethical values accommodate to a drastically altered age distribution? What will be the effects upon successive groups of young, and what will be the eventual effects upon their old age (Neugarten, 1973)?

Do we then resolve this by interpreting Kant's words: "Man . . .exists as an end in himself, not merely as a means for arbitrary use by this or that will. . ." *(Groundwork of the Metaphysics of Morals)*.

Care for the aging had reflected the growth of civilized human society. There has been considerable progress from the time when people were expendable because of the culture of the times, some religious practice, or failure to be productive. Even the dread workhouses and human storehouses have been left behind. There is today a truer appreciation of the elderly as an integral member of humankind and the efforts to give them status and respect, while caring for their social and physical needs, continue. The strategy of the religious institution should be to fit the service to the individual, not the individual to the service; it should be an operative network providing options and alternatives which extend the capacities of the elderly and their families; and, thus, enhance the lives of the elderly through a consummate fulfillment of their humaneness.

REFERENCE NOTES

1. Kaplan, J. The institution as the cornerstone for alternatives to institutionalization. In *The Gerontologist,* February 1974, *14,* No. 1, p. 5. The early publications listed therein were authored by J. Kaplan.
2. Genesis, XII, 6.
3. Deut. X, 14.
4. Talmud, B.B. 8 b.
5. Ruth, IV, V5.
6. Exodus XX, 12.
7. Josephus, "Ant" XXII, Sec. 5.
8. Philo, "de Caritate": Sec. 12.
9. Julianus, "Epist" XXX, 49.
10. II Kings XV: II Chrm. XXVI, 21. For greater detail, the reader is invited to pursue the article, Development of care of elderly: Tracing the history of institutional facilities by J.G. Gold and S.M. Kaufman in *The Gerontologist,* 1970 *10,* No. 4, from whence most of the historical references and detailed writing contained herein was drawn. Appreciation is expressed to *The Gerontologist* and the Gerontological Society of America.

References

Curran, C.E. (Ed.). *Absolutes in moral theology*. Washington, D.C.: Corpus Books, 1968.

Dupre, L. Natural end and natural law. *Contraception and Catholics: A new appraisal*. Baltimore: Helicon, 1964.

Hartman, L.E. Retribution, *Encyclopedic dictionary of the Bible*. New York: McGraw-Hill, 1963, Col. 2032-2036.

Kant, I. Groundwork of the metaphysics of morals. In *The Moral Law*. J.J. Paton, trans. London: Barnes & Noble, 1948.

Maves, P.B. Research in religion in relation to aging. *Proceedings of Seminars*—1961-65. Durham, N.C.: Council on Gerontology, Duke University, 1965, pp. 69-79.

Neugarten, B.L. Patterns of aging: Past, present and future. In *The Social Service Review*, February 1973, *47*, No. 4, p. 579.

Seneca: *Epistles, epistle LVIII*. Cambridge: Loeb Classical Library, Harvard University Press, 75:407, 1967.

Chapter 10

HOSPITAL CLERGY AND
THE ELDERLY PATIENT

Carleton J. Sweetser

I am the chaplain of a large acute-care general hospital complex, where the length of patient stay is primarily a short one, and where I regard ours as a kind of crash ministry to human beings in the midst of acute crises, of intense but short-term pastoral involvement in their lives. They are the acutely sick, the seriously injured, the dying, and their loved ones, often the newly bereaved. Our mission is to help them through immediate pain, terror, or loss, usually just to the point of the beginning of "recovery," whether the emphasis be on physical wholeness or spiritual equanimity. It has seemed not so much a ministry to the whole fabric of peoples' lives, which would appear to have more to say to their aging (but I'm not so sure and will come back to that later); rather, to a critical but limited portion of a life, or cluster of lives.

But I serve on the board of a neighboring residence for the elderly, now becoming more and more a skilled nursing facility (a professional and polite way of saying "nursing home") as well as on the related board of a fund which, thank God, is able to provide some services and activities that make life a good bit better in the home, and offers, too, stipends and other assistance to retired and elderly people

136

otherwise not able to go on living independently in their own homes.

Not long ago some of us in the community were shocked and angered by the sudden dismissal, by a young, very efficient, and I'm afraid not very sensitive administrator of another residence for the elderly, of a devoted, conscientious, sensitive, patient and empathetic chaplain, for what I'm convinced were personal, small, and not valid reasons. I've never visited a patient from there (for their sick come to our hospital), who when asked if he or she were acquainted with the chaplain, didn't respond with, an indeed, yes, that the chaplain was the best and most appreciated friend they had there, that he was one who really understood their problems, was often their one channel of hope in difficult hours, and that they wouldn't know what they would do without him. The abrupt termination didn't permit even a day for goodbyes, the semblance of a graceful withdrawal, or personal termination of longstanding pastoral relationships that meant so much to so many residents, to say nothing of a sixty-two year-old chaplain himself. I continue to hear of those bereft elderly, still mourning the loss of the chaplain.

As I have been trying to concentrate on the concerns and needs of the elderly from the perspective of a hospital ministry, I have become more and more aware of my own impending sixtieth birthday this year. I am an individual who still likes to ski and sail, and whose self-image is very much of one youthfully active, albeit with an occasional bursitis, stiffness of joint, cold or infection that seems to take a little longer than they used to to clear up. This birthday is weighing surprisingly heavy on my mind. *Ageism*, the prejudice against the elderly in our culture Dr. Robert Butler (1975) describes so tellingly[1], certainly has some real roots in our own reluctance to join the ranks of the elderly. It can express itself in curious and devious ways, indeed, in one who tries to minister sensitively to all the sick. All of a sudden it's not so much *I* and *they*—the *chaplain who ministers* and *the elderly in the homes and the older sick in the hospital*—but an unavoidable and growing sense of *oneness*, that one knows intellectually is appropriate and should be creative, but which, too, is emotionally frightening, depressing, and needs coming to terms with if both mininstry and life are going to be meaningful and whole from here on.

A special concern for many of us in recent years has been the *hospice*—the appropriate and meaningful medical care and support of those in the terminal stages of illness and their loved ones, a desperate and long ignored need. St. Luke's, I'm so grateful to be able to say, has for almost 6 years operated a hospice program increasingly accepted and used by our medical staff, that has to date cared for some 500 patients, 470 of whom have died; and many have lived longer, most more comfortably and fully, have spent more time out of the hospital, have died at home or during brief final admissions, than would have been the case had they not been hospice patients. C.G. Jung[2] writes

> Natural life is the nourishing soil of the soul. From the middle of life onward, only he remains vitally alive who is ready to die with life. For in the seçret hour of life's midday the parabola is reversed, death is born. The second half of life does not signify ascent, unfolding, increase, exuberance, but death, since the end is its goal. The negation of life's fulfillment is synonymous with the refusal to accept its ending. Both mean not wanting to live; not wanting to live is identical with not wanting to die. Waxing and waning make one curve (p. 6).

Jung meant every bit of natural life—to its very end—as all-important for the life and growth of the human soul, and is why hospice care for the dying is so necessary.

In my own one serious illness and hospitalization, I was deeply grateful to find—and here hospice work helped—that I could accept death, if it was to be the outcome, with spiritual equanimity, not morbidly, but trustingly. It has made a difference in ministering to the dying and acutely ill—an empathy that was not there is quite the same way before; and I recommend one serious illness for every doctor, nurse, administrator, and other serious minded care-givers, including clergy.

But what about Jung's natural life as the nourishing soil of the soul in terms of years of older life with all its possibilities for chronic and painful ailments, loss of physical independence, gnawing loneliness, curtailment or ending of activities that have meant so much, and all the rest that we, perhaps especially in the health care field, willy-nilly think of as the sickness of old age? (For myself, I know there is work to be done, perhaps quite overdue—an aging self to be gotten a lot more in touch with— if ministry to the elderly sick is going to be genuine). Getting in touch with the reality of one's own dying is vital to good care of and ministry to the dying. Getting in touch with aging through our own aging selves is equally necessary to ministering to the elderly, especially the sick. With death it is at least beginning to happen, after years of scientific and sophisticated denial, pretense, and neglect, thanks to hospice. But with the aging process I don't believe it is happening much, especially in our hospitals where the elderly and chronically ill (86 percent of the over sixty-five population) (Butler, p. 175) are far from being the most "interesting," "promising," "exciting," and wanted patients.

Centuries ago the Psalmist[3] cried from the depths of the soul of the sickness, guilt, grief, loneliness, and social treatment of old age:

> Have mercy upon me, O Lord, for I am in trouble;
>   my eye is consumed with sorrow and also my throat
>   and my belly.
>
> For my life is wasted with grief, and my years with
>   sighing;
>   my strength fails me because of affliction, and my
>   bones are consumed.
>
> I have become a reproach to all my enemies and even to
>   my neighbors, a dismay to those of my acquaintance;
>   when they see me in the street they avoid me.
>
> I am forgotten like a dead man, out of mind;
>   I am useless as a broken pot.

Or again,

> I said, 'Lord be merciful; heal me, for I have sinned
>   against you.'
>
> My enemies are saying wicked things about me:
>   'When will he die, and his name perish?'
>
> Even if they come to me, they speak empty words;
>   their heart collects false rumors; they go outside
>   and spread them.

'A deadly thing,' they say, 'has fastened on him; he
has taken to his bed and will never get up again' (Psalms,
41:4-6, 8).

And finally, the poignant prayer,

For you are my hope, O Lord God, my confidence since I
was young.

Do not cast me off in my old age; forsake me not when
my strength fails. . .(Psalms, 71:5, 9).

"Do not cast me off in my old age; forsake me not when my
strength fails." And how we do this in our culture, and our health
care system so geared to "acute care," scientific "miracles,"
dramatic and satisfying physical successes. Good chronic care—appropriate treatment of long term illnesses, stabilization instead of
continuing deterioration, mental and physical adjustment to perma-
nent limitations, as well as very possible reversal of diseases of the
elderly—demand sophisticated, up-to-date, sensitive, painstaking,
and unhurried health care, but are concerns that too often wind up in
the 'custodial' backwater of the care system. I remember, in a planning session for a hospice symposium at a great medical center, a
distinguished surgeon demonstrating that we must not "waste" these
valuable beds on these people (in the terminal stages of illness), and
yet there is probably no hospital with greater potential for controlling
pain, or capacity for medically enhancing the lives of people in their
last days. I firmly believe that true acute care is the right care for the
right person at the right time. Both terminal and chronic care must be
in the mainstream of medicine, research, and the concerns of all of us
who care for the sick if the system is going to be whole.

To bear strong witness here, to bear witness to better human
priorities and to a different and transcendent set of values, is a role
that hospital clergy must play if they are truly to minister to the elderly sick and contribute to the hospital's true mission of wholeness for
all. Getting in touch with one's own aging self, beginning to accept
with trust that waxing and waning make a single curve in one's own
life, as I'm somewhat painfully discovering myself, is essential. To
see in the beautiful imagery of Henri Nouwen and Walter Gaffney

(1976) the wisdom of God and one's own unique worth as a spoke in the wheel of ongoing creation—ascending first and then descending but always equally a part of the wheel in its eternal forward motion (pp. 13.ff.); to begin to be in touch with a self that will more and more find its meaning and joy in being and reflecting rather than the achieving and producing our culture values so highly, and a gentle letting go of the seeming all-important goals and roles of the ascent that need no longer pressure and enslave one, I believe is the way of good aging. To accept with trust, live more and more in touch with this kind of life, is the quiet but assuring witness desperately needed in the maelstrom of the modern hospital, by its elderly sick, their perplexed families and loved ones.

Then, a growing sense of mutuality with the elderly sick, their grief, their guilt, their pain, their many losses in life, their limitations and rejections, in an activist culture (including its medical component) can happen. Brother Roger (1973), the Prior of the great lay Commmunity of Taize in France, writes beautifully of his work with the many young people who come there searching, but speaks equally to me of our ministry to the elderly in the hospital:

> I know from experience how hard the first contact with them can be. To begin with they are on their guard in the presence of (those) bearing the charge of authority; the first question is often abrupt. They need to test the temperature of the man who is here before them. . . .And there can be no running away from this; what counts is to listen, so that trust can break through (p. 11).

To listen is what counts, so that trust can break through. To listen with love, patience, and acceptance to the "garrulousness" of the elderly so often born of their social loneliness, and with interest to reminiscing that really can tell us so much about who the person is and bring new insights to the listener. Trust can break through and with it the growth of a healing relationship—healing that is both ways because only as we receive can we give. And with trust can come the unburdening of the guilt of a life, the assurance of forgiveness, which is the giving of new life, and often a vital factor in the healing of sickness.

Several years ago the gracious old residence for the elderly, where our chaplains also serve, was replaced by a much larger and modern facility. In the confusion of that transition the beloved furnishings of the old chapel were temporarily lost, and it was only after much needling of the administration by a persistent resident who had long assumed the care of them that they were finally found. As a relieved administrator and the chaplains were unpacking and preparing to arrange them in the present chapel, I knew this wasn't right and allowed that we should call the lady in question before proceeding further. The administrator disagreed, explaining patiently that a first principle of geriatrics is to go ahead, take the appropriate action for the elderly, and afterwards present it as already accomplished in their own best interests. I replied that it was not a first principle of mine, insisted that she be called; she was thrilled, worked with us, and it is once again the chapel that is important in her and many other residents' lives.

A distinguished social worker tells me of the hospitalization for acute emphysema of her husband's eighty year-old father, a bright and alert gentleman, who after building and retiring from his own successful printing business, continued an active intellectual life, writing and publishing articles in retirement magazines, but who in his present physically weakened condition is treated increasingly like a helpless child by his nurses. "Be a good boy, David;" "Now eat your supper like a nice boy," are the admonitions in the high-pitched, supercilious tones associated with the cajoling of little children, and sadly this brilliant and able man is responding more and more as a dependent child.

"The individual becomes morally and spiritually inferior in the mass," Jung (1958, p. 56) pointedly reminds our society. For institutions to be quick to make and present to them as *faits accomplis* decisions about the daily lives and interests of the elderly, for nurses and other hospital care-givers to infantilize their older patients, for an administrator brutally to deprive his sick and elderly residents of a relationship that meant so much in their lives, for medical staffs to see their elderly sick as uninteresting and trying relics to be pushed so quickly out of the mainstream of medical care into what is called professionally "custodial care" (but medically often meaning *hopeless*)[1] is to consign human beings to the mass of agism and indeed make them morally and spiritually inferior: to say nothing of what it can do to them physically.

But it is the uniqueness of each individual as a child of God—that which in every person, no matter what age or mental or physical condition, is always the same self, the inner image of the Creator—and the all-importance of the present moment of one's being which, regardless of the attendant circumstances, may well be the most important in that lifetime as it fulfills its God-given destiny, that I believe are the concepts for a valid ministry to all human beings. These concepts become critical with respect to the elderly in hospitals. To be able to accept, with trust that even the so-called senility manifestations in some, which terrify us now, which we're quick to assign to the elderly and nervously make insensitive jokes about, can have even their healing and protective function for a life outwardly drastically curtailed, yet which in the deeper mystery of being, is ever the same person. It made my sister, with whom my mother lived at the end of her life, unhappy because she missed the former relationship; but our mother, earlier bold, active, and creative, who would have been terribly unhappy in the full awareness of limitations, I know was happy in her own withdrawn life, and to us, imaginary world. One of our ablest and most concerned doctors in this area spoke to me of the great need of modern medicine to understand the viable treatability of many of the mental syndromes of the elderly, the need likewise not to disrupt the peace and protection that mental withdrawal brings to some of the old, and the need to distinguish sensitively and appropriately between the two—certainly, a challenge for ministry to the elderly in hospitals, and to their families, and to their care-givers.

And finally, to be allowed and enabled to live and die as one's self. I often think of a dear friend of the chaplains at Bellevue Hospital, a lovely West Indian woman, whose life radiated a trust in God and love of people and who spent her waking hours as a tireless volunteer in the hospital. Suddenly diagnosed with a tumor of the colon, colostomy was prescribed as the only way to save her life. She refused, and in the face of urgent pleas by her doctors, signed herself out of the hospital, with this explanation: "I am over eighty. I have had a very full life for which I am most grateful. All these eighty-plus years I have moved my bowels in the orthodox manner. It is too late for me to change. If I were young, with my life ahead of me, or if my children weren't grown, it might be a different matter. I am ready for whatever my Lord has in store for me. She did, to satisfy them, agree to return periodically for examinations. I believe those chaplains felt that they had never known a person of more trusting faith. And the tumor disappeared. Her complete trust opened her to every possibility, a trust so deep that it really didn't matter to her at that point whether she continued to live physically or went on to what lay ahead in God's eternal scheme, which, to my way of thinking, is complete healing.

I'm a great believer in the *ministry of the laity*—of these concerns and this ministry belonging to us all. I know of no area in life where the ministry of the laity can be more truly practiced than in that of medical care and our institutions of healing. The clergy, perhaps, have at special times and in connection with special needs of God's children, the responsibility of helping other care-givers understand and be more fully and completely God's ministers in the many facets of their service to their fellow human beings. I would borrow and direct this challenge from Nouwen and Gaffney's beautiful little book, *Aging,* to all medical care-givers today:

> What seems the most frightening period of life, marked by excommunication and rejection, might turn into the most joyful opportunity to tell our community top from bottom. But who is the one who will take their fear away and will lead them out of the darkness of segregation, desolation, and loss of selfhood into the light which is prepared for all nations to see? Who is that young man who will have the courage to step forward in his society and proclaim that by ostracizing the old men the traditions will be lost and a series of disasters could take place? (p. 86).

Reference Notes

1. R.N. Butler, *Why survive? Being old in America.* Harper Colophon Books, 1975, p. 11, ff; Chapter 7 The unfulfilled prescription.
2. See Jung, C.G. The Soul and Death. In Herman Feiful, *The Meaning of Death,* McGraw Hill Paper Books, 1965, p. 6.
3. Psalms, (Psalter Translation): The Book of Common Prayer. New

York: The Church Hymnal Corporation & The Seabury Press, 1977, Psalm 31:9-12.
4. Butler, see Chapter 7, The unfulfilled prescription.

REFERENCES

Jung, C.G. *The undiscovered self*. Atlantic-Little, Brown, 1958.
Nouwen, H.J.M. & Gaffney, W.J. *Aging*. Garden City: Image Books, Doubleday, 1976.
Roger, Br. *Festival*. New York: The Seabury Press, 1973.

Chapter 11

RELIGION AND THE SIGNIFICANCE OF THE EXPERIENCE OF DEATH

Donald F. Clingan

I. INTRODUCTION

Just as the realities of aging are universal among us, sooner or later we must face the reality of death coming into our lives through those whom we know and love, and finally to ourselves. Are we ready and willing to face this challenge?

There are many reactions to death.

A grandmother died at one hundred seven years of age in Indiana. At one hundred five she had remarked, "Well, I can die in peace now. All of my children are in nursing homes."

Then there was the elderly woman whom we'll call Mary. Mary had known for several months that she had terminal cancer. Her family and friends knew of her impending death. Yet there seemed to be an aura of victory round about her. She was the epitome of courage.

One day her friend, Bill, seeing this spirit, remarked it. "Mary, you radiate such a sense of triumph and courage. How can you be so brave?"

Mary replied, "Bill, I've spent most of my life showing my children how to live. Now I must show my children how to die."

So are life and death interrelated, intertwined. Do we, through the vibrance of our lives, reveal our religious faith (whatever that faith may be) and in that revelation show those around us the significance of facing our own death for achieving vital day-by-day living? In other words, have we faced our own death from the gut-level to the point that we are finding the fullness, the richness of life?

II. FACING MY OWN DEATH (TO FIND LIFE)

I was fifty years of age, 5 years ago, when I determined to better prepare myself for effective *ministry with* the *aging* by pursuing a Doctor of Ministry degree. One element I knew to be lacking in my life was obvious. I had never been helped to face my own death from the personal feeling level.

I had taken the usual seminary courses in the theology of death and funeral practices. I knew, at least to some degree, about autopsies, bequeathing parts of the body for medical purposes, choices in disposition of the body, the duties and knowledge of a funeral director, embalming, types and places of memorial services and ministries needed by the family and friends in grief. I had dealt with death from the viewpoint of an intellectual head-trip. I had dealt with death quite well when it came to others—my friends, my family, even my mother and father. But to deal with my *own* death, my *personal* death—this I had not achieved.

I began to search for some situation where I could learn to face my own death from the gut-feeling level. At that time I could find no seminary which could help me. I did find an internationally renowned seminar on *Confrontations with Death* offered at the University of Oregon, in Eugene.

The seminar was limited to 40 persons and conducted for 5 concentrated days, Monday through Friday. To be accepted in the seminar, you had to go through a stringent application procedure. The experienced and highly trained leadership involved knew the limitations and potentialities of the seminar. For instance, those with recent death and grief experiences could not be admitted because of the trauma that might be involved.

When the seminar first began, we met as a total group of 40 for several experiences in confronting the realities of death. One period involved sharing with a young man who was pronounced terminally ill with cancer and now found himself in remission. We heard the testimony he offered about the emotional stages he faced in dying which we have learned to know through the research of Kubler-Ross (1969):

Denial and Isolation
Anger
Bargaining
Depression
Acceptance

Our comprehension was enriched by music which he had composed in these different emotional stages.

Yet soon the large group, through a meaningful process, was divided into groups of eight that became for us our "family" in common quest, in common confrontation with death.

I can remember my group:

a Roman Catholic Sister;
a young man who was a Ph.D. candidate and a professed atheist;
a grandmother who was a person of real Christian faith;
an older man who was a funeral director;
a young man who was a funeral director and who had obviously not faced his own death;
a young woman working in the field of aging;
a young woman of the "flower-child culture" who served as a professor of recreation in a California university;
and myself,—a national church executive.

We were led by two trainers in some meaningful depth experiences. It is impossible to describe them all, but I will share some of the key moments.

Early in the week we were asked to take a long sheet of paper and create our own "life lines"—beginning with our birth, showing our ups and downs in life experiences, and then projecting when we would die, how we would die, and where we would die.

We were all going to die when we were in our 70s or 80s. No one was going to die sooner. And yet, how did we know we would not die tomorrow? We didn't.

To share our lives in depth with each other caused laughter and tears, joy and sadness; but in the end it was an experience of release, enrichment, and growth.

Another day we were asked to write our own obituary and epitaph. What would you like for those with whom you have lived to remember about your life? I remember that I projected that my life would end with a heart attack while I was mowing my lawn at home. Other facts are blurred in my memory.

The day before the seminar was to close, each of us in our small group was appointed to die. When my turn came, I lay down on the carpeted floor in the midst of my group in the small room where we were meeting. My eyes were blindfolded and I was completely covered with a sheet. For all intents and purposes I was dead to my group.

Before I died I had given my self-written obituary and epitaph to a young man in the group whom I had learned to appreciate as a person and as a friend. Now that I was dead, I heard my friend read my epitaph and obituary. Then the group began to share their deepest feelings about what my life had meant to them while I had lived among them.

I laughed, I cried, I felt about every emotion there was to feel. Then it occurred to me—what if I should die tomorrow? What if I could never hold my wife, Jacquie, again in my arms and tell her how much I loved her? What if I could never hold my children close again and say, "Hey kids, I love you!" How many times had I been too busy being a "national church executive" to *be* with my family and express through my life how important they were to me?

And then the words of Jesus became very real to me—

If you would save your life, then you are going to lose it. But if you lose your life for my sake, you will find it (Matthew 10:39, RSV).

I determined as I lay under that sheet that from that time forward I would sincerely seek to make every day count in my life, for I did not know when death would come for me. In facing my own death

from the gut-level, I found out how rich, how complete, how rewarding life can be.

In the midst of my moments of renewal, I heard someone in my
group say—"Well, how shall we bring Don back to life?" You see,
the group had to determine how they would bring me from death to
life. They decided that they would lift me up bodily as a group until I
could touch the ceiling.

When I came back to life from that experience, having faced my
own personal death, I really came back to life; and I've never been
quite the same!

To me, facing our own death and its interrelatedness to life in
light of our religious faith gives us a new light in facing three important and basic life questions. To deal with these questions in depth
because of the reality of death in our existence can enrich our lives.

III. THE BASIC QUESTIONS OF LIFE
(WHEN I FACE MY OWN DEATH)

A. The first basic question of life you and I must face when we
experience the reality of death is the functional one—

Who am I?

Before God, who am I?

I talked with a friend this week. We'll call her Judy. Judy is a
medical writer, a wife and a mother. She is a woman full of life, more
than she had ever realized. Last December Judy discovered she had
breast cancer. Examination also revealed involvement of the lymph
glands under the left arm. Since then she has undergone surgery and
now has begun extensive chemotherapy treatments which she will
need to continue for at least a year.

As I talked with Judy, I felt life had taken on a new meaning for
her. She knew, in a new way, who she was. She announced that
because she was facing her own death, she was finding new expressions of life. She said:

> I feel alive. I really feel I'm an instrument for a special and
> unique task. I feel guidance and have accepted the task of be-
> ing a National Director of an Education Program on Cancer
> for my religious faith. . .What is so gratifying is the love that

has been shared with me out of this death–life experience. I'm in the good hands of my doctors, but they also have loving hands. I feel the love of my family and friends more than I have ever before. I have learned that when you give, you gain more strength. . . My learning desire and capacity seems extraordinarily heightened. My insights are marvelous. The creative energy I'm feeling is most exciting.

This is Judy's experience of finding who she really is and what potential she really has in God's sight (as she has faced her own death).

Are you willing to face the question *Who am I?* in the light of your own faith and the reality of your own death?

Dr. Nevin C. Harner (1950) in his book, *I Believe* was most perceptive when he indicated that we can see ourselves from at least three perspectives (pp. 40-50).

First, we can believe that we are no more than 5 or 6 dollars' worth of iron, phosphorus, calcium, carbon, and the like, recognizing that prices are going up in these inflationary times. This is the *drug store* answer for who we are.

Secondly, there is the *scientific answer* which turns to biology, physiology, psychology, etc., for a more respectful estimate of our life's value. Through science we can see the marvels of our human bodies.

For example, we know that

a digestive apparatus takes in food of various kinds, grinds it into bits, adds the proper chemicals at successive stages, and transmutes it into energy. . . .

A few pints of blood course endlessly through arteries and veins, carrying nourishment to every cell, and carrying off waste products.

The heart contracts and expands, minute after minute, year after year—the most perfect engine the world has ever seen.

A delicate thermostat holds the body temperature at approximately 98 degrees in winter and summer, indoors and outdoors, rarely fluctuating by a fraction of a degree.

The human brain may be likened to the central

switchboard of a telephone system, with innumerable wires running out in various directions . . .(Harner, 1950, pp. 41-42).

Recognizing all these miracles and more, is this all we are—a scientific phenomenon? No, there is a third and more paramount answer that comes out of our life–death experience and our religious faith.

Who are we? We are children of God. It is the conviction of the Judeo–Christian tradition that we are made in God's image. We are called by God to share in ongoing creation as his creatures, co-creators in covenant with him. We are valuable because we are vessels of God's ongoing revelation.

Kenneth Caraway (1976) said: "Life is made for freedom of spirit. And that freedom includes what I can do with my boxes. There is no box made by God nor us but that the top can be blown off and the sides flattened out to make a dance floor on which to celebrate life" (*Newsletter,* Fox Valley Older Adult Services).

In our self-centeredness, we may create boxes that cause us to stagnate in life and die while we are still breathing. Yet we have the power given to us by God to turn anger into love,

> guilt into hope,
> sin into salvation,
> fear into challenge,
> conflict into peace,
> darkness into light,
> death into life.

B. In this light, we need to face the second basic question of life coming out of our experience of the reality of our own death. That question is—

What is my life purpose?

Do I have a reason for living as I grow older and even when I become very old? Do I have a reason for living when I'm lying in a nursing home or a hospital bed? Is there a unique ministry which only I can fulfill in the light of my gifts and experience?

I am more and more convinced that God sees older persons as being not automatically but potentially "His Splendid Ones," giving of themselves in unique ministry through church or synagogue and community. Our task at any age is to see this potential and enable it to happen in our lives and the lives of others.

Knowing that death is a reality for you, what do you see as your life purpose?

In the words of Henri Nouwen and Walter Gaffney (1976):

Aging is the gradual fulfillment of the life cycle in which receiving matures in giving and living makes dying worthwhile. Aging does not need to be hidden or denied, but can be understood, affirmed, and experienced as a process of growth given to us by God by which the mystery of life is slowly revealed to us (p. 4).

An anonymous poet has written:

> Age is a quality of mind.
> If you have left your dreams behind,
> If hope is cold,
> If you no longer look ahead,
> If your ambition's fires are dead —
> Then you are old (and dead in life).
> But if from life you take the best,
> And if in life you keep the zest,
> If love you hold —
> No matter how the years go by,
> No matter how the birthdays fly,
> You are not old (but alive)!

C. This brings us to the third basic question of life we need to face which comes out of the experience of the reality of our own death. This question is —

How can I live my life to its fullest? or

How can I fulfill my life most completely?

I first became acquainted with *four principles for good adjustment in growing older* through Dr. John Brantner, a Clinical Psychologist and Professor of Psychology at the College of Medical Sciences, the

University of Minnesota in Minneapolis. Since then I have grown in my conviction that just as these principles have a strong research base, they also have a strong base in religious faith, at least in the Judeo-Christian tradition.

Dr. Brantner notes that the four principles also are —

> well based in controlled studies,
> basic to being old and "being O.K.,"
> central to good adjustment in life,
> associated with control of blood pressure
>   and have a clear effect on physiology,
> can be taught,
> can be memorized in a minute, but must be worked
>   on for a lifetime.

I would add that these principles, in my judgment, can enable us to live life to its fullest and can enable us as we face the reality of our own death to find out potential in life as "God's Splendid Ones."

And what are these principles?

1. The first one is to *be open*. This means that we need to find someone we trust—this may or may not be our spouse, may be a friend, a family member or a counselor—and share our distress. We need to be effective complainers, but not constant gripers. We need to give our burdens away, not being on the defensive, but being assertive, being ourselves comfortably. In the words of some psychologists, we need to "get the garbage out"—all of our angers, fears, pain, resentments, concerns—so that these barriers within us may be broken down to release us to be the whole persons God created us to be.

2. The second principle for good adjustment as we grow older, a principle that can help us as we face the reality of our own death to find life in its fullness, is to be *light-hearted. Celebrate life and death.* Let the good news of your religious faith capture your very being. Avoid despair, depression, and hopelessness. This does not mean to avoid sadness and grief. We know that we must work through sadness and grief. We have learned this through Kubler-Ross (1969) and Westburg (1962). However, once we recognize the difference between sadness and depression, we can avoid that depression by searching for cheerfulness, picking the roses instead of complaining about the thorns.

This is our task if we are to celebrate life.

3. The third principle for good adjustment as we grow older, a principle that can help us as we face the reality of our own death to find life in its fullness is to *keep active,* in every way—mentally, physically, emotionally, and spiritually. Dr. Brantner reminds us that we need to do more and more when our energy is waning, and that more than normal bed-rest cannot benefit a person physically (except perhaps in heart cases). We need to learn to stay active. When we resist activity we deteriorate. When we keep active we come alive.

A woman who died at ninety-three years of age observed shortly before her death that her only prayer would be that "I will wear out and not rust out." We need to keep active.

4. The fourth principle for good adjustment as we grow older, a principle that can help us as we face the reality of our own death to find life in its fullness, is to *reach out to others.* This means that we need to behave in an extroverted way, remaining sociable and adding acquaintances at every opportunity. We need to learn to talk to strangers, avoiding isolation, alienation, and loneliness. Loneliness is simply the lack of meaningful relationships. When we reach out to others in concern, we develop these important relationships.

Dr. Karl Menninger, the famous psychiatrist, after giving a lecture on mental health was answering questions from the audience. "What would you advise a person to do," asked one man, "if that person felt a nervous breakdown coming on?" Most people expected Dr. Menninger to reply, "Consult a psychiatrist." To their astonishment he said, "If you feel a nervous breakdown coming on, lock up your house, go across the railway tracks and find someone in need and do something to help that person."

Every community, city, or rural area has its "railroad tracks" that seem to lay down boundaries over which you will find those persons who are in need. We have the spiritual need to reach out to those persons for their sakes and for ours. We need in our lives to be enabled to give as well as to receive, to be involved constructively in ministry with others insofar as we are capable.

Most of us as we grow older are physically and mentally able to give of ourselves. If we are wise, we recognize our spiritual need to give for others as well as to receive, even when we are limited like Frances.

Frances is a double amputee living in a Los Angeles nursing

home. Both of her legs are amputated. One day she said to her pastor, "What could I do for our church?" the pastor asked for time to explore this request. He frankly admitted that his chief concern had been for what the church could do for Frances rather than for what she could do for the church. But he soon returned, and among other suggestions, he said, "Frances, you could be responsible for the 'cheer ministry' in our church. You can send get-well cards, anniversary cards, birthday cards, condolence cards, and all the kinds of cards that need to be sent. If your task becomes too big, you can use the telephone at your bedside and recruit other nursing home residents or shut-ins from our church to help you." Frances became excited with the idea and said, "I'll do it!"

Later, I had the privilege of visiting Frances and I asked her if she really did all that had been reported to me. She replied, "I surely do, but I did have a friend come to me recently and say, 'Frances, you shouldn't be doing all these things. You should be ministered unto rather than ministering.'" Frances reported that she looked her friend in the eye and said, "I ain't dead yet!"

IV. CONCLUSION

Perhaps all I have sought to share about religion and the experience of death that leads to life can be summarized in a simple hymn by Avery and Marsh (1971). Facing the reality of our own death can give us new life,

> new opportunities for living,
> new joy in our existence.

We can come to life through death with the fresh approach of a little child facing each new day.

> Come as a little child,
> Come with a smile of eagerness.
> Greet each new day as a special gift of love.
> Even if you're old and gray,
> Though you've come a long hard way.
> Come ready to sing and play and dance,

Ready to risk and take a chance,
For of such is the Kingdom,
For of such is the Kingdom,
Come as a child.

REFERENCES

Avery, R.K., & Marsh, D.S. *Come as a child*. Port Jervis, New York: Proclamation Publications, Inc., 1971.

Harner, N.C., *I believe*. Philadelphia: The Christian Education Press, 1950.

The Holy Bible, Revised Standard Version. New York: Thomas Nelson and Sons, 1952.

Kubler-Ross, E. *On death and dying*. New York: The Macmillan Company, 1969.

Newletter, Fox Valley Older Adult Services, Serena, Illinois. March 1976.

Nouwen, H., & Gaffney, W. *Aging: The fulfillment of life*. Garden City: Doubleday & Company, Inc., 1976.

Westburg, G. *Good grief*. Philadelphia: Fortress Press, 1962.

Chapter 12

THE ROLE OF THE CHURCH
IN THE COMMUNITY

Thomas C. Cook, Jr.

"Why," asks Paul Maves (1980), "should the churches be interested in the field of aging especially?" And then he asks, "How should the church be related to the field of gerontology, or related to work with the aging? (p. 51). The answer to the first question ought to be obvious, for while every ninth American is at least sixty-five years old, (Brotman, 1981 p. 2) the church (and we can include synagogue in most references to church) is graying at an even greater rate than the population as a whole. "Church" is people; and if a large segment of your people are older adults, fifty-five years of age and older, some attention must be given to their special needs. In 1959 I graduated from the seminary and recall the senior class interviews by pulpit committees. In those days, the question that sticks out in my mind had little to do with beliefs or biblical knowledge or preaching ability. The committees asked, "Can he (or she) work with the young people?" That was a relevant question to ask, as anyone who remembers the 60s knows. But, I submit that an equally important question should now be posed in view of changing demographics during the last 20 years or so—"Can he (or she) work with older people?" Relevance in our day requires that we be prepared to say *yes*!

The question of "How should the church be related to the field of gerontology?" is, of course, the next logical issue to be grappled with.

What is the role of the church? What is that role in the community? What is community? How do we relate these to aging and older persons?

To speak of a "role" is to state the appropriate or customary function of anything. But "church," in all of its scope, history, and traditions, is like looking at both forest and trees. And we must relate the matter of characteristic and appropriate function to aging and then to that function within the community.

First, what is a community? The German philosopher and sociologist, Tonnies (1855-1936), is credited with distinguishing (Christensen & Robinson, 1980) between "the two absolute sociological categories: community and society (p. 14), community being the personal in forms and society the more general. Delespesse (1968) provides us with a good definition of community:

A community is a union of human beings held together by an underlying principle. The underlying principle unites the members in their very persons and not only in their activities or material goods (the result of which are merely a society), and makes them come to know and love one another. This knowledge and love is concretely expressed in a sharing at all levels (spiritual and material), in a mutual support and in a certain common life (p. 6).

This definition is somewhat restrictive. Of course, Delespesse's focus is on what might characterize the church itself or a religious order. In everyday life ours is a less precise use of the term. But community, as a segment of society, is the part of the world where we live and relate and require covenants of behavior essential to our own family unity and well-being.

In the Greek language we recognize "fellowship" or *Koinonia* as the origin of the term community. New Testament writers see community both as an integral part of and result of the celebration of the eucharist.

Much interest in our day is centered on the secular field of community development or "CD." Christenson and Robinson (1980) in

Community Development in America have reviewed the roots of civilized community, beginning with Aristotle who asserted that people found community as the setting in which mutual associations could be enjoyed, basic needs fulfilled, and where meaning in life could be discovered. Thomas Hobbes, the philosopher, took the position that community was the natural outgrowth of people serving, in a group setting, their own self-interest. "Community allowed individuals to abandon the many diversified and labor-demanding activities required in subsistence living. By coming together in a community setting, one individual could be a farmer, another a baker, a third a merchant, and so on. Men and women could pursue, within certain limits as defined by customs and mores, the activities suited to their ability and/or liking (Christenson & Robinson, p. 5).

Such views on how community or communities form may be true in so far as they go, but they do not go far enough. Community is more than economics or protection or specialization or self-fulfillment, though all these may take place in such an environment. Community will not long exist without some common values which transcend the material and external. Historically, what we may now describe as church or synagogue is a community. Clingan's (1980) handbook, entitled *Aging in the Community of Faith,* qualifies community in terms of these values.

Just recently at the NCOA Annual Meeting, I chaired a panel on Wholistic Aging in which one speaker dealt with the subject *Changing Times and Unchanging Values—Faith Perspectives and the Older Person.* This theme is one we must grasp if we are to understand how to minister effectively, not only to the elderly, but to all ages in our pluralistic, changing society. We need a community which cannot be destroyed by external conditions, socioeconomic roller coasters, and current events. The writer to the *Hebrews* spoke of Abraham "seeking a city which has foundations whose builder and maker is God" (Heb. 11:10). In other words, people of faith always seek for a community the qualities and characteristics of which are always greater than the sum of its social and economic parts.

The ancient tribes of Israel, the modern Jewish kibbutz, the religious monastic orders, congregations, and the parish depict community formed around unchanging, transcendent but relevant, and, yes, "revealed" values.

It is this community within the greater community, this sacred society which, however weak, however small, is the nucleus around which whatever social order there is exists.

Frances Schaeffer (1976) says, "If society has no absolutes, then society itself becomes the absolute." One role of the church is to be prophetic and keep the revealed absolute values demonstrated before secular society. Where this fails, where we turn to purely humanistic designs for living, however good these seem, eventually we arrive where that ancient society, reported in the Book of Judges, found itself when left to itself: "And every man did what was right in his own eyes"—and we read that there was chaos in those days (Judges 17:6, 21:25).

"Church" is a word derived from the Greek word *Kurioke* and means "those who belong to the Lord." In scripture, church is the leaven of society—the change agent which, when it practices what it proclaims, is the redemptive instrument to the total society.

But if the people of God are the changers of the social order, who changes the church? Any first-grader knows it is God who does that: But experience and scripture show how much we who believe try God's patience before we obey.

The political surprises of November 1980 signaled a desire for sweeping change—any change—by the voting public. Whether it is indicative of a forthcoming revival of faith or not, the pendulum of social and family life-style is about to swing back. The question is whether it will be triggered by practical necessity, or by war, or economic disaster, or by the movement of the Spirit of God within his people? One religious possibility is stated in the formula: "If my people who are called by my name humble themselves, and pray and seek my face, and turn from their wicked ways, then I will hear from heaven, and will forgive their sin and heal their land" (II Chronicles 7:14).

Shubah, Hebrew for "turn" or "repent," signals the beginning of change, and is the religious element which is the dynamic that triggers energy in the church to be relevant in and to society.

We have evidence for the demographic realities. The problem of the church is in awareness, relevance, and redirection of resources, energy, and commitment to these facts.

What then does all this mean in terms of aging and the church?

Simply that the role of the church must be relevant, consistent with the espoused values, and that ensuing action be empathic, specific, and true to our belief in the dignity of the individual.

I have had the privilege of serving as Consultant and report writer for the Technical Committee on Spiritual Well-Being of the 1981 White House Conference on Aging. For this and other reasons, those who read the report of that committee and the Report of the mini-White House Conference on Aging convened by the National Interfaith Coalition on Aging *A Symposium on Spiritual and Ethical Value System Concerns in 1981 WHCOA,* may discover a natural, and not contrived, resonance.

These two reports identify important issues of great concern of the religious community as it looks at national policy formulation in the 1980s. I shall highlight the overarching issues of these documents here.

National or Collective Role

Because the religious sector comprises one of the largest constituency groups in the United States, it was important that the role of churches, synagogues, and other religious organizations be addressed in the 1981 White House Conference on Aging. The 1971 White House Conference on Aging, through a section on spiritual well-being, enabled many concerns of the religious community to be raised and addressed. Theological and philosophical values embedded in the concept of spiritual well-being need to be looked at with the intensity afforded by such a special section. On the other hand, spiritual values cannot be compartmentalized. Ethical values and matters of the human spirit related to service delivery and policy affecting older Americans permeated most major issues dealt with by the 16 WHCOA technical committees (Fahey, 1981).

In the non-sectarian, pluralistic sense, national policies in aging and human services in general will find support from the voluntary and religious sector as programs and resources for older Americans are provided in a way that recognizes the importance of spiritual well-being to total well-being. For this reason it is urgent that the Older Americans Act, as well as private sector and religious foundation funds, be made available to research spiritual well-being (Fahey, 1981).

Previous White House Conferences have enlisted vigorous support from persons concerned with the spiritual needs of older Americans. The resources and commitments of the religious sector have been evident. The creation of the National Interfaith Coalition on Aging, a volunteer coalition of 31 religious bodies, to respond to the 1971 White House Conference on Aging recommendations in the area of spiritual well-being and to the report as a whole has had significant impact on the field of aging in the past decade. This continuing exploration of the mission of the religious sector in the field of aging has extended to the surveying of 111 national denominational offices and more than 135 seminaries and schools of religious education (Cook, 1976).

In 1975 this Coalition developed an interfaith definition of spiritual well-being: "Spiritual Well-being is the affirmation of life in a relationship with God, self, community, and environment that nurtures and celebrates wholeness. Within this group of religious bodies, commitments to ministry both with and for the elderly have increased in the past decade and many have formulated position or policy statements (Cook, p. 89).

A Wholistic Approach

Aging in the United States takes place in a society so pluralistic, fragmented, specialized, bureaucratized, and secularized that matters of the spirit—the moving and integrating force in life and personhood—are largely ignored. The result is that aging, which should and could be crowned with integrity, acceptance, wisdom, and fulfillment, is too often characterized by aimlessness, loneliness, hopelessness, and despair. To change this condition, wholistic well-being, inclusive of spiritual well-being and its associated values of human dignity and freedom, should be the chief unifying goal of all social action, public and private, that is directed toward the aging (Group Report from The National Symposium, 1981, p. 1).

"Wholeness," or the wholistic (holistic) is inherent in the notion of spiritual well-being, of which there can be little without some movement toward wholeness. This was a clear point of the Spiritual Well-being Technical Committee.

Spiritual well-being and religious experience are often sidelined as optional or peripheral. A wholistic view of the individual, on the other hand, sees him or her as a functioning being, coordinating vitally the physical, emotional, intellectual, spiritual, and social dimensions of life as an inextricable totality. Change in one dimension affects the whole. Neglect of one dimension diminishes all. Support of this view of the individual requires a resonant response from society to organize its functions, processes, services, and policies in support of wholeness (Group Report, 1981, p. 1). National policy must therefore include all aspects of life experience, including the spiritual.

If we lack definition or clarity, or feel uncomfortable with the spiritual as part of the whole of life, we must all the more include it in our research and service goals to improve the total well-being of older persons. This approach requires that both secular and religious sectors not speak of "wholeness," nor of the "integrated," or "total person" when the spiritual aspect of life is omitted from consideration.

There must be national policy which reflects the importance of making provision for the spiritual well-being needs of all age groups, but especially older people. The religious sector must promote this if it is to be done.

The second major point identified by the Technical Committee is that religious institutions have a role as architects of societal attitudes.

Religious institutions form one of the largest groupings of American society; and, as advocates for the elderly, they are capable of bringing awesome pressure to bear on decision and policymakers to produce creative change. On the other hand, as many concerned individuals and groups rightly point out, the status quo often persists because church and synagogue do not live up to their own Judeo-Christian standards (Gray Panthers, 1980). Life fulfillment is seriously curtailed in a culture where attitudes, policies, and programs place restrictions on the aging person's opportunities for self-expression, improvement, and involvement.

The decades of the 1960s and 1970s have seen profound changes in the values and belief systems in our nation, especially as these relate to changing roles of women and men, family structure, attitudes toward the young and old, and changes in modes and fashions of worship. These changes and those in our economy and lifestyles effect our values and attitudes and are reflected in national policy. One of the greatest challenges facing religious institutions is the reshaping of societal attitudes and the redirection of social trends so critical to the achievement of an age-integrated society. The religious sector characteristically speaks to its own members, and through them infuses its values and standards into the disciplines and service domains of our society.

> The central credo of most. . .traditions. . .while variously expressed, is the unqualified worth of persons as persons created by God, whatever their age or station. This conviction applied to the lives of older persons in a community enables church and synagogue to enhance, through their own channels and resources, the quality of life for all ages, as older persons make contributions and also receive ministry commensurate with their real condition, talents, and meaning in current American life (A Statement of Philosophy and Purpose, 1980).

As proponent of the personal worth of the individual and the wholeness and fulfillment in each person's life, the religious sector can act as a unique catalyst in guiding society toward a more just and humane policy in aging.

The third major point related to the role of aging has to do with religious institutions as providers of service. Religious institutions like the family and other agencies are mediating structures in American society. Particularly, local congregations provide a place of identity, belonging, and refuge, support rights of the individuals, and, at times, facilitate the individual's relationship to power structures. Such mediation ranges from advocacy on behalf of older people to services to assist in self-care or total care of the person, as needed.

Historically, both institutional and community-based services by and for older persons have been created and operated under religious auspices. Adult day care, senior centers, residential homes, nursing and health care centers, and a variety of personal support services of a "hands-on" nature gives substance to espoused concerns. With a growing number of vital older persons not in institutional care or in need of specific services, denominational programs logically extend the life-enrichment opportunity and involvement of older persons as volunteers in the service of others.

Just as important is the need to include other adults in the life, worship, and social activities of the congregation. While institutional services of a public or private nature tend to be more formal and structured, religious institutions are uniquely equipped to provide services of an informal nature through congregations to meet many of the needs of elders in the community.

In a technological age, where productivity and family mobility accelerate, norms are not established for accompanying societal changes. In many cases old values are displaced in the wave of change, leaving ethical decisions and societal values to operate on expediency. Organized religious bodies can help preserve dignity in aging by mediating and supplementing programs established by every level of government. They may also properly influence national policy.

The fourth point identifies the role of religious institutions in meeting spiritual needs of the elderly. "The concerns and resources of communities of faith for their aging are as old as the communities themselves. Church and synagogue contribute directly to quality of life of the aging by fostering spiritual well-being. . ." (A Statement of Philosophy and Purpose, 1980). By definition, spiritual well-being moves beyond specific religious arenas to the wholeness of the individual and the quality of life. The religious community provides a milieu in which concerns for the spiritual needs of older adults may be nurtured and enhanced. While spiritual well-being applies without regard to age, the vicissitudes of growing older provide unique opportunities for spiritual growth essential to wholeness in the individual.

Acknowledgment of the spiritual nature of persons can put the trials and satisfactions of life into a sane perspective. The spiritual cannot be separated from the physical but rather transcends and permeates life to give it its fullest meaning. Thus spiritual well-being and spiritual values have a bearing on the total personality and total society.

It is precisely at the point of acknowledgment of the total needs of older people that the religious sector may address the whole of society, speaking effectively to the phenomenon of aging and aiding in the fulfillment of persons and the humanization of bureaucracy and technology. It is equally important that the religious sector, through its congregations and agencies, encourage the aging to continue giving to society from the wealth of their experiences and to remain active participants in community life.

Meeting the needs of older persons in the 1980s requires greater understanding of processes of aging, especially dying and death. Emphasis must also extend to promoting lifelong spiritual and intellectual growth. Such must be the curricular foci within both religious and secular training and educational programs to make more competent those who serve the needs of older Americans.

It needs to be repeated here that spiritual needs permeate all social, psychological, and physical needs of older persons. Policies and programs of religious institutions must respect needs of older persons as persons, not just remote objects of study and interest. Attention to their needs requires not only minds and hearts, but hands and legs. Doctors may rarely make house calls in our day, but congregations can and should!

However religious bodies define their own spiritual and theological mission, older persons must receive such ministry in terms of their own faith. Whether through sacraments, scriptures, worship, or other familiar means of grace, churches and synagogues have a responsibility for outreach, inclusion, and spiritual succor to older congregants.

Though spiritual and ethical values are somewhat amorphous and difficult to assess, they nevertheless are wellsprings for all human services—public and private, secular and religious. Moberg (1973) sharpened this perspective and pinpointed a research dilemma:

Since spiritual well-being is infused into all of life's activities, experiences, feelings, attitudes, beliefs, organizational programs and the like, it is very easy to miss its central significance at the very core of human nature. Also, since a kind of "spiritual blindness," according to the Bible, inflicts people who lack spiritual enlightenment, those scientists and scholars who are non-believers in God can adopt as an unspoken posture a denial of the essentially spiritual nature of man and will refuse to observe evidences of the ontological reality of the spiritual component in human nature. There

are indeed great complexities related to the subject, but if the
religious bodies do not give attention to spiritual well-being,
no other major institution in society will (p. 3).

The biblical prophet Joel speaks of the young having visions and
the old dreaming dreams (*Joel* 2:28). Whatever age-integration
means, it calls for the gifts of the young and old to be acknowledged and
employed. But Joel's words on dreams and visions, also echoed in the
New Testament (Acts 2:17), follow prophecy. A better community
and a better society for all age groups will see not only a "foretell-
ing," but a requisite "speaking-forth" prophetic call. While this is a
traditional role of religion, it is also the spiritual legacy of our U.S.
Constitution. Values guarded by constitutional fiat are designed to
benefit all without tests of age, means, race, or creed. Any trend
toward the ultimate solution of the needs and problems of this decade
or the next will require a values-coherent and values-practicing society. In this respect, the government has a protective and legal role.
At the same time, the religious community must apply its prophetic
role if the quality of life in any "age-integrated" social system is to
flourish and permit dreams and visions to have meaningful expression.

We are reminded by Dr. C. Welton Gaddy (1980) that the application of values in national policy formulation will not be easy:

Inevitably, the conscience on aging revealed in the religious
community's pastoral concern will come in conflict with the
conscience on aging evidenced in the secular community.
However, tension at this point can be very beneficial (p. 11).

This tension, he asserts, accompanies all significant social
change. It is therefore incumbent on church and synagogue to be persistent in challenging prejudices, the status quo, and in demanding
redress of wrong. Together, secular and religious sectors must provide an ethic by which policies and programs in aging may be
evaluated (Gaddy, p. 19).

The church approaches the community, then, from a perspective
of hope and from the basic values and faith most Americans share.
Much in the spirit of Rabbi Abraham J. Heschel's address to the 1961

White House Conference on Aging, Welton Gaddy (1980) raises a positive challenge:

> We have much to offer the aged. Problems can be attacked. However, we have much to obtain from the aged. Promises can be realized. The presence of the elderly can help stabilize our communities and be a source of strength in our families. Their memory can bind us to our heritage and teach us to learn from the past as we plan for the future and the present. Their wisdom can challenge our disoriented lifestyles and call forth a reassessment of those matters which are ultimately important—human relations, promises to keep, personal affection, and similar concerns. Their experience can inform us on how to live better with less in the face of inflation. Their faith can inspire our faith to the point that we share their hope. . . .
>
> The aged hold great promise for our society if we will but have the good conscience to lay hold of it. Our manner of response will be indicative of our humaneness or beastiality; our sense of integrity or lack of it. Judgment on our feeling about and interactions with the aged may take the form either of blessing or condemnation. All of the evidence is not yet in (pp. 19, 20).

The Fourth Gospel of (John 19:26, 27) records that Jesus, in one of his solemn moments on the cross, in the shadow of the mighty act of the redemption of mankind, paused to assign to his dearest disciple the care of his mother. Surely, those of us who taste the fruits of that redemption cannot, in good conscience, abandon the fifth commandment, "Honor thy father and thy mother that thy days may be long in the land which the Lord thy God giveth thee." Jesus rebuked many religious people for avoiding that kind of care and honor by tying up their money in otherwise respectable and religious offerings (Mark 7:8-13).

At the heart of that caring which lifts us all to God is the natural caring for young and old, without which redemptive love loses its human authenticity.

Ultimately, there is no real community where there is no fullness of life for those who reach the fullness of years. The *Shema* (prayer in the book of Torah) says "You shalt love the Lord your God with all your heart, and with all your soul and with all your mind—"

Jesus links with that the commandment "You shalt love your neighbor as yourself" (Matt 22:37-40; Deut 6:5; 10:12). Our *neighbor*, as well as our *self*, is growing older. The question is, can we love?

References

Brotman, H. The aging society: A demographic view, *Aging,* January-February 1981, *315-316,* (U.S. Dept. of Health and Human Services), p. 2.

Christensen & Robinson, (Eds.), *Community development in America,* Ames, Iowa: The Iowa State University Press, 1980.

Clingan, D.F. *Aging persons in the community of faith.* (Rev. ed.) St. Louis, Missouri: Christian Board of Publication, 1980.

Cook, T.C. Jr., *The religious sector explores its mission in aging.* Athens, Georgia; National Interfaith Coalition on Aging, Inc., 1976.

Cook, T.C. Jr., *et al. An age-integrated society: Implications for spiritual well-being.* Washington D.C.: 1981 White House Conference on Aging, Background and Issues Report, Technical Committee #12, p. 11.

Delespesse, M. *The church community, leaven or lifestyle.* Ave Maria Press, 1968.

Fahey, Msgr. C.J. Ethical implications for a greying society. Paper presented at the National Symposium on Spiritual and Ethical Value System Concerns in the 1981 White House Conference of Aging, Cincinnati, Ohio. National Interfaith Coalition on Aging, Inc., 1981.

Gaddy, C.W. Aging: *A call for conscience.* Address, National Interfaith Coalition on Aging, Ninth Annual Conference: Aging and Spiritual Well-being: Issues of Consciousness, Conscience, Commitment, Competence and Care, Washington, D.C., May, 1980, p. 11.

Gray Panthers Testimony, *Hearing on American Values in National Policy.* National Symposium on Spiritual and Ethical Value

System Concerns in the 1981 White House Conference on Aging. Athens, Georgia: National Interfaith Coalition on Aging, Inc., October, 1980.

Group Report from the National Symposium on Spiritual and Ethical Value System Concerns in the 1981 White House Conference on Aging, Athens, Georgia: National Interfaith Coalition on Aging, Inc., 1981, p. 1.

Heschel, A.J. The older person and the family in the perspective of Jewish tradition. Paper presented at the 1961 White House Conference on Aging, Washington, D.C.

Maves, P. Spiritual well-being of the elderly: A rationale for seminary education. In T.C. Cook, Jr. & J. Thorson, (Eds.) *Spiritual well-being of the eldery*. Springfield, Illinois: Charles C. Thomas Publications, 1980.

Moberg, D. *Spiritual well-being:* Background and issues for the technical committee on spiritual well-being. 1971 White House Conference on Aging, Washington, D.C., U.S. Government Printing Office, 1971, p. 3.

Schaeffer, F. *Spiritual well-being. A Statement of Philosophy.* from *How Shall We Then Live?* (Film Series).

————. *Spiritual well-being: A definition.* Athens, Georgia: National Interfaith Coalition on Aging, Inc., 1975. (One page definition and commentary).

————. *A statement of philosophy and purpose.* Athens, Georgia: National Interfaith Coalition on Aging, Inc., 1980. (One page statement).

Chapter 13

ORAL HISTORY
Accounts of Lives and Times*

G. Cullom Davis

In a famous essay, C.P. Snow[1] argued that the sciences and the humanities were so dissimilar as to be two separate cultures. Whatever the ultimate accuracy of his opinion, there are occasional and important exceptions to it. One of these exceptions is the burgeoning field of oral history, which clearly represents the convergence or intersection of the scientific and humanistic cultures. In the past 25 years, there have been independent trends in one of our youngest social sciences—gerontology—and one of our oldest humanities—history—that have brought these otherwise alien fields together into a common endeavor. That common endeavor is oral history. What are the independent developments in each field that have intersected, accounting for the development of oral history?

In the field of gerontology, there have been important clinical activities and writings by psychiàtrists and psychoanalysts on the developmental stages of life and especially the concept of the "life-review" as a universal mental process. The leading student and exponent of "life-review therapy" has been Robert N. Butler, former Director of the National Institute on Aging.[2] Others have added to the literature.[3] These individuals have spoken of the life review or reminiscing as a potential positive act for the elderly and even as a technique in individual and group psychotherapy. Butler (1963) refers to life review as a natural healing process. Whether on their own or in therapy, older persons can review their entire lives recognizing the continuities and discontinuities in those lives, resolving old personal conflicts, facing some of the dark corners, and thereby come to terms with what their life has meant and what it can mean. The result, according to Butler and others, is not some sort of unrealistic retreat into the past but rather a very healthy and realistic sense of oneself in one's time and in one's place as well. Life review therapy, therefore, enhances the elder's ability to face the present and to deal with the future. One authority in the *Journal of Gerontology,* Charles Lewis (1971), has even suggested that this life review activity may contribute to longevity in older people.[4] Whether or not one accepts that argument, it is clear that gerontologists have focused attention and research in recent years on the beneficial and therapeutic effects of reminiscing by older people.

What about history? What has happened to this discipline in the last 25 years that draws it close to gerontology? I refer to two trends. One of them is the subject matter that historians study and the other is the method that we use to study it. Historians in recent decades have been busy rediscovering subjects that have been around for a long time, but were overlooked. In the 1960s, for example, we quickly and suddenly rediscovered poverty, even though poverty had been around for a long time but had been concealed by the veneer of postwar abundance. After that, we rediscovered black Americans, Indians, women, and recently we have rediscovered the older American. I refer to some interesting recent articles and books that demonstrate that finally and rather tardily, American historians have begun to look at the elderly as historical objects and as historical agents. Works by David Hackett Fischer, Peter Laslett, John Demos, David Van Tassel, Andrew Achenbaum and Tamara Hareven stand out among the important work being done in my field on the subject of aging and the aged.[5] So our subject matter has grown now to embrace older Americans. What about the method, that second trend in history? In order to gather information about these long forgotten and neglected people, the poor, women, blacks, and older Americans, we cannot employ the conventional historical sources that we use to study presidents and other elites. We cannot use archives or collected letters or newspapers very effectively. Therefore we must turn to technology to recapture and to reconstruct the lives of these people. The technology we turn to consists of the computer and the tape recorder.

With the computer, quantitative historians amass and sort mountains of statistical data that describe the general behavior of entire populations. The computer enables these quantitative historians to make gross generalizations about the sameness or common characteristics of human behavior. An example of such a generalization might be, "Eighty-three percent of southern farmers did not own land in 1930," and such a statement would be based on statistical sampling of census bureau and tax data.

The tape recorder is very different from the computer. With the tape recorder, we collect not mountains of statistics, but rather anecdotal reminiscences. These materials describe not the general behavior of populations, but the distinctive singular behavior of individuals. The tape recorder enables us to portray in rich detail not the sameness, but the differentness or uniqueness of human behavior. An example might be the intimate life story of a southern sharecropper. There is such an oral autobiography, and I recommend it.[6]

Of course, it is the tape recorder that I'm talking about in oral history. Oral history is a technique for gathering eye-witness personal recollections about the past. It consists of the collection, processing, preservation, and dissemination of personal reminiscences by trained historian-archivists. There are some recent books in oral history that deal pointedly with senescence and the lives of older people. One is Don Gold's *Until the Singing Stops,* a collection of some 20 oral histories of older people. Another, which is almost lyrical in its prose, is *The View in Winter: Reflections on Old Age,* by the British historian Ronald Blythe.[7] Here is what Blythe (1979) says about old people: "It is the nature of old men and women to become their own confessors, poets, philosophers, apologists, and storytellers" (p.29). That is exactly what Blythe succeeds in doing with the life stories of some 37 people he interviews in this book. So the otherwise alien and dissimilar fields of gerontology and history have converged in recent years on a common practice—the life review as gerontologists call it, or oral history, as historians call it.

Our work may converge, but that does not mean that our purposes, techniques, and accomplishments coincide. It is important to understand how oral historians and gerontologists differ in their common quest for the reminiscences of older people. First and most fundamentally, our goals in collecting reminiscences are very different. The oral historian is seeking information by tapping a precious historical source. Our aim, which may sound cold to gerontologists, is to get older people's recollections on tape before it is too late. In that work we are driven by what we oral historians sometimes call "the actuarial imperative." That is to say we are haunted by the obituary page because every death means the elimination of one potential historical source. Our interest, one must remember, is in historical information.

The gerontologist has a far different purpose as I understand it. The gerontologist is providing therapy or assistance. He or she is serving rather than using; trying to help older people live happier integrated lives. Expressed most simply and bluntly, the historian uses interviews to *take information from* older people, while the gerontologist uses interviews to *give assistance to* them. Just how sharply contrasting could our goals and purposes be? Of course the results and the processes may be identical; the oral historian inadvertently helps and the gerontologist inadvertantly collects information. But such byproducts are extraneous. The fundamental difference is illustrated by a second contrast. Oral historians refer to their subjects as informants because they are seeking information. Gerontologists refer to their subjects often as clients. The same individual may be an informant or a client, depending on who interviews them.

The third difference has to do with the qualifications to perform this work. Oral historians believe that interviewing requires extensive historical knowledge and training in technique; but we would not dream of expecting counselor or psychoanalytic credentials in our interviews. That is what gerontologists expect. In turn they ignore, and understandably so, historical skills as unnecessary and irrelevant. Robert Butler (1963) has said that anyone can conduct life-review interviews, and he has even called for a "National Listeners Corps" of volunteers—a mass grassroots effort—to enlist people simply to listen. Here too is a deep difference in our respective activities as to the qualifications for performing them. But this deep difference is somewhat mitigated by our apparent agreement on one overriding behavioral qualification. We all seem to agree, we oral historians and gerontologists, that the successful interviewer must be a good listener and must be empathic. Still, these three differences divide our efforts and carry potential problems as we pursue our work independently.

One of those problems is that historians are wary about the informational value of recorded life-reviews, because they have been collected by individuals whom we regard as historical novices. No doubt gerontologists have similar concerns about the therapeutic value of our work. There is also a legal and an ethical issue that can be a problem in the separate work that we do. Historians seek to use interviews, perhaps publish them, and certainly to disseminate them as widely as possible. They are, after all, supposed to be information, and our purpose is to share and to use information—the more widely, the better. Therefore, we routinely secure a legal release for every interview we collect. Counselors and psychiatrists have professional expectations and standards that require them to observe strict confidentiality in a client-counseling relationship, so that there is some divergence on the legal and ethical plane between our interviewing activities.

There is also the delicate problem of taboo or sensitive subjects in a person's life experience. As I understand it, the therapist focuses on these taboo or sensitive subjects: focuses on them to help the client explore and resolve them as a part of the healing process. Oral historians avoid or drop these taboo or sensitive subjects unless the informant is freely willing to talk about them, in which case they are not taboo. In citing both these differences and these potential problems, I do not mean to imply that they are irreconcilable. On the contrary, my readings and my own personal experience convince me that our shared values far outweigh our differences in actual practice. Let me cite two cases to demonstrate how well oral historians and life-review gerontologists work together.

One notable example of the genuine merger of the oral historian and the gerontologist is a program conducted by the Senior Citizens Center at St. Alban's Parish in Washington, D.C. They were inspired in their work both by Robert Butler and by the oral history work represented by *Foxfire*. They were advised both by gerontologists who were experts in life-review therapy and by professional historians who were experts in oral history. The volunteers at St. Alban's Parish collected some 100 personal histories on tape. Their avowed purpose was both therapeutic and informational. They even published an interesting book on the subject—a combination sampler from the interviews and a technique manual for others to follow. It is called *Past Present: Recording Life Stories of Older People.* It was written by Sara Jenkins, who was director of that project, and is available from the National Council on Aging.[8]

The second example of successful collaboration and merger is more personal and occurred in central Illinois. It is described briefly in a newspaper article entitle *Talking History.*[9] Several years ago Josephine Oblinger, then director of the Illinois Department on Aging, conceived a novel plan to use CETA funds to employ older persons in four Illinois counties to interview other older persons. The venture had an avowedly dual purpose: to gather historical information and to serve older persons. Accordingly, both oral historians and gerontologists were involved throughout the venture. In my judgment, it was a substantial success and was further evidence of our common interest and our shared values. Both social service and social science were served by the older persons whom we selected, trained, and supervised. They helped fellow elders explore their life histories while they served Clio, the Muse of history, by gathering historical information. Thus the same program yielded both therapy and history.

I have worked actively in the field of oral history for 10 years. In addition to teaching the subject to university students, I also founded an oral history archival program which employs 10 persons and currently offers some 1200 hours of recorded interviews (30,000 pages of transcript) for research by historians. I have conducted many interviews and supervised the production of hundreds of others.

What did this oral history work teach me about older people and about the life-review process as we understand it? Very early in my labors and long before I read the works of Robert Butler, I discovered the mutual benefits that both parties to an interview can realize. For me as the interviewer, the work was interesting and immensely gratifying, and it kept creating new friendships that otherwise would never have existed. For the informants, as we call the people we interview, the experience was clearly and consistently a positive one. They enjoyed the work. They wrote thank-you letters. Some of them volunteered to help after they had been interviewed. Many purchased extra copies of their oral histories to give to relatives and friends and many became close and enduring friends. Clearly and emphatically oral history was a positive experience for them. This serendipitous development—spreading happiness while collecting history—pleased me, but to be honest it also made me uneasy. For one thing the notion of helping people while engaged in research was alien to my scholarly training in my field. Moreover, I was troubled that unintended good will might also have its opposite, unintended injury or disappointment for older persons. Was there some potential backlash effect in oral history? I did not know, but I remember making it a point to caution my students and my interviewers to maintain a very proper, businesslike relationship with their 'informants so as to avoid any future misunderstandings or disappointments on the part of those older persons. I have now concluded that these fears were totally groundless. The oral history interview is an inherently and a uniformly positive experience for older persons—just as Robert Butler later told me it was—so long as the practitioners conduct themselves as responsible, empathic listeners. As I see it, oral history's benign and therapeutic qualities stem from the following:

Our informants understand that our interest and inquisitiveness about them is genuine, not patronizing. We want to use them, and that is a gratifying discovery for them. Moreover, some of our informants may have few material possessions left in the world, but their memory is one possession they can generously share and yet still retain. Third, informants discover that their life experience has meaning, not only for themselves, which is what Robert Butler has pointed out, but for countless others who may study and learn from it. The recognition that one's life story has meaning for untold generations to come can be a very rewarding sensation. And finally, informants perceive their oral history as a tangible legacy or gift to their families and to posterity. Some may even view it as some sort of monument or a measure of immortality that they gain. In short, oral history imparts dignity, stature, self-respect, and significance to older persons.

There is one feature of the oral history or life review interview that strikes me as particularly interesting for gerontologists. That is the question of closure. How do oral histories end? What an informant says or fails to say at the end of a long life-review may be significant. I have not done a systematic study of this, but I can identify several kinds of characteristic closing to our oral histories of older people. Some interviews end very abruptly. Some of them even dangle at the end. They appear unfinished to any reader or listener. In fact, some are unfinished. We have a good many interviews that we think are over, and periodically, after we have finished, the informant will telephone or write us that he or she has thought of something else that they might like to add to the story, so that the story keeps unfolding. Other interviews end very naturally, with finality, but without any particular flourish or lifetime summation. A good many interviews end this way with the interviewer saying, "Is there anything else or any final thoughts you wish to share about your life and your career?" The informant will say, "No, I can't think of anything." And that is it. But at least there is closure to that interview even though it is not particularly reflective or summative. Finally, a few informants, being perhaps more conscious of the testament that they are creating, carefully compose a closing statement. This statement sometimes resembles a kind of premature epitaph or summation of the focus or the meaning of their life. I want to describe two of them that particularly interest me as examples. One of them is from an interview we did several years ago with a local black physician, Dr. Edwin Lee. Dr. Lee chose to end his 100-page memoir with a public event at which he was honored as the city's outstanding citizen. He chose this event to symbolize his lifetime struggle to become a physician and to overcome racial prejudice. Let me read from Dr. Lee's closing statement.[10] He talks about being fooled into coming to the awards breakfast.

> I was a bit stunned when my name was called, and I was escorted to the rostrum by two previous winners. I must say that that was certainly a thrill to stand there and be acclaimed as the Copley First Citizen of Springfield, Abraham Lincoln's hometown, and I think I felt that it was at this moment that much of the work that I had done was coming to fruition in the fact that there had been a change in this town, looking back over 23 years, having known when black people were not welcome as guests in their hotels and any other places of respect. Then here I stood, through no particular accomplishment of my own, but certainly through a change in attitude and the help of many people, I was being acclaimed

the number one citizen. So here we are, in 1973; and until the next First Citizen, I am enjoying that distinction, having come a long way from Indianola, Mississippi. This is the end (p. 111).

With that very touching statement Ed Lee's oral history ended. Clearly he chose that event as symbolic of the meaning of his life.

My second example concerns a gentleman whom I had the good fortune to interview. His name was Henry McCarthy. Henry was a very unusual man: a person of intellect and executive skill who achieved international recognition and high office in his field of social welfare administration. He and I worked for a year to put some 40 hours of his reminiscences on tape. The result is a 500-page oral autobiography of some 300,000 words. It covers Henry's life in rich detail, from his Irish Catholic boyhood in Massachusetts and Rhode Island through schools and Catholic seminary to graduate study at the University of Chicago. His career in social work is well known among those in his field. He was the first regional director of Social Security for this tri-state area in the 1930s and perhaps the youngest one ever to hold such a major federal office. For 10 years he held the exalted position of New York City Commissioner of Public Welfare, the top metropolitan welfare job in the world. He then "retired" and moved back to Illinois and became an Assistant Director of the Department of Public Aid where he directed the Aging Section that distributed federal funds for local senior centers. Then he agreed to help launch the embryonic Illinois Department on Aging in 1973, and assisted the first directors, Harold Swank and Irving Dilliard. He knew and vividly remembered people like New York Mayor Robert Wagner, Averell Harriman, Eleanor Roosevelt, and others.

Henry agreed to be interviewed because he had a keen sense of the history of his time and of his personal role both as an agent and as an object of that history. His memoir freely reviews both his successes and his failures, the high points and the embarrassments, his satisfactions and his regrets. And how did this great man of many accomplishments choose to end this rich 500-page memoir? He closed by recognizing the culminating position in his career as that of welfare commissioner in New York City, but he also added this humble reflection:[11]

Now, if you want something else that I always like to add to this; I think that all of that pales into insignificance, and I sometimes wonder whether all of it was worth what it sounds like when I speak about it, compared to the fact that I sired two sons, and have seven grandchildren. Perhaps my greatest contribution to the world would consist of the fact that I fulfilled my biological function. And that possibly, in the evolutionary process some of my genes, as they influence the equipment which my descendants will have, will in this great genetic sweepstakes sometime result in another Einstein, another Oppenheimer, another Lincoln, somebody; that is something that gives me satisfaction.

There is a poignant postscript to Henry McCarthy's oral history. After we finished this marathon interviewing, and my typist had begun producing transcript pages, Henry continued to give this project great effort and thought. He painstakingly reviewed every page of transcription for errors. The enterprise consumed countless hours of work and became so important that he made arrangements for his wife Harriet to carry on the work if necessary. Sadly, that did prove necessary. Henry McCarthy died in 1979. He died quickly and quietly in his favorite haunt—the public library—doing what he loved to do—reading, writing letters, and toiling on his oral history. His death was a great personal blow to me, because by virtue of our detailed and intimate conversations I had come to love and to admire him. But I also knew that by any measure he had led an extraordinarily full, productive, and vital life and that its richness had continued literally to the instant of his death.

By coincidence, just hours before he died, Henry had written a long, typically interesting, and reflective letter to a mutual friend, Irving Dilliard, a distinguished journalist and constitutional authority. One passage in the letter pertained to Henry's oral history:

Dear Irving:

Every spring, as I look out the window of our apartment at the burgeoning leafy boughs of the trees, I automatically resort to prayers of thanksgiving to the Eternal God that I have been granted the gift of life for another spring—and of hope that I may be here to see another one a year from now. I spoke with Cullom yesterday. I'm nearly finished with my own editing of my oral history. The transcription runs to more than 600 pages. It is the hardest work I have ever done. I feel so frustrated—as I go through each chapter and realize how much I left out!—to me I seem to have given a most superficial account of the events of which I was a part for the past 77 years. I think I did not even begin to scratch the surface, and was guilty of being too anecdotal and rambling, like a garrulous old man. The temptation to rewrite and extend my remarks is very strong, but this is exactly what Cullom and his staff don't want me to do. They prefer the raw spontaneity which is the distinguishing feature of the whole oral history concept. . . .All and all, although it has taken a lot out of me, it has been an enjoyable experience, and I hope you, Irving, will too when you get into it with Cullom. (Letter dated May 25, 1979; copy in author's possession)

A few hours after writing that Henry died suddenly while at work on his own oral history. His experience with the life-review process is but an example—albeit a touching and persuasive one—of the significance of oral histories in the two alien fields of gerontology and history. Creating a personal reminiscence clearly was an important and constructive activity in Henry's final years. Even in his last days and hours it motivated him, it frustrated him, it consumed and occupied him, and quite evidently it also pleased him. At the same time, the gift that he gave to us is priceless. It is a unique and informed perspective on the past 70 years and a rich treasury of eyewitness experiences that some day will be published in book form. In other words, doing an oral history enriched Henry McCarthy's own life and enriched our historical understanding.

These examples illustrate and suggest the value of reminiscence to gerontologists and historians. We seek different objectives and we apply different expectations and criteria, but our separate disciplines converge in putting the reminiscing capacity and habits of older people to good use.

REFERENCE NOTES

1. Snow, C.P., *The Two Cultures and the Scientific Revolution*. New York: Cambridge University Press, 1963.

2. Butler, R.N. The Life Review: An interpretation and reminiscence in the aged. *Psychiatry*, 1963 *26*, pp. 65-76; Lewis, M.I. & Butler, R.N. Life-review therapy: Putting memories to work in individual and group psychotherapy. *Geriatrics*, November 1974 *29*, pp. 165-69, 172-73; Butler, R.N. Successful aging and the role of life review. *American Geriatrics Society* November-December 1974, pp. 529-35; Butler, R.N. *Why survive? Being old in America*. New York: Harper & Row, 1975.

3. Menninger, R. Some psychological factors involved in oral history interviewing. *Oral History Review*, 1975, pp. 68-75; Meyerhoff, B. & Tufte, V. Life history as integration: An essay on an experimental model. *The Gerontologist*, 1975, p. 541; Meyerhoff, B. *Number Our Days*. New York: E.P. Dutton, 1978; Kastenbaum, R. . . .Gone Tomorrow. *Geriatrics*, November 1974, pp. 127-34; Lieberman, M.A. & Falk, J.M. The remembered past as a source of data for research on the life cycle. *Human Development*. 1971 *14*, pp. 132-141.

4. Lewis, C.N. Reminiscing and self-concept in old age, *Journal of Gerontology*, 1971 *26*, pp. 240-43.

5. Fischer, D.H. *Growing old in America*. New York: Oxford University Press, 1977; Aschenbaum, W.A., *Old age in the new land: The American experience since 1790*. Baltimore: Johns Hopkins University Press, 1979; Hareven, T. & Langenbach, R. *Amoskeog: Life and work in an American factory city*. New York: Pantheon, 1978; Van Tassel, D.D. (Ed.). *Aging, death and the completion of being*. Philadelphia: University of Pennsylvania Press, 1979; S.E. Spicker *et al* (Eds.). *Aging, and the elderly: Humanistic perspectives in gerontology*. Atlantic Highlands, New Jersey: Humanities Press, 1978.

6. Rosengarten, T. *All God's dangers: The life of Nate Shaw*. New York: Alfred A. Knopf, 1974.

7. Gold, D. *Until the Singing Stops: A Celebration of Life and Old Age in America*. New York: Holt, Rinehart & Winston, 1979;

Blythe, R. *The view in winter: Reflections on old age.* New York: Harcourt, Brace, Jovanovich, 1979.

8. Jenkins, S. *Past present: Recording life stories of older people.* Washington, D.C.: St. Alban's Parish, 1978.

9. Koplowitz, H.B. Talking History: Litchfield senior interviews seniors about the past. *Illinois Times*, April 14-20, 1978.

10. Quoted from *Edwin Lee Memoir.* Sangamon State University Oral History Office, 1973.

11. Quoted from *Henry McCarthy Memoir.* Sangamon State University Oral History Office, 1980.

Chapter 14

RECREATION
An Expression of the Art of Living

Virginia Lee Boyack

There are certain attitudes that have been described by the Canadian educator, Dr. John A.B. McLeish (1976) as qualities that are typical of older individuals experiencing the art of living:

> . . .consider that life is a process of continuous growth, as much through the later and very late years as in any earlier period; that the capacity to learn is fully operative among human beings across the entire span of life, and that one simply goes ahead and learns, and grows; that human creativity comprises, apart from the splendours of genius, thousands of manifestations of the mind and imagination which transform an individual's own self or his or her environment; that creativity cannot be taught and learned as one can teach and learn a language; but that certain conditions, all of them potentially available in later years, can be fostered so that the creative attitude and powers, on whatever scale, can be liberated. The most important of these conditions are maintenance of a wonder toward life, openness to

experience, the sense of search, and scope for the best of the child-self which is present in all of us (p. 285).

As McLeish further notes that most older adults:

. . .enter the later years with such conventional lifestyles and attitudes, their individual identity so diffused—or confused—and their powers of creativity so unused and rusted, that only by a gradual process or by the intervention of some revolutionizing event in their lives can new capacities for growth and creativity emerge and begin a transforming process (p. 286).

I am reminded of words from Tennyson's poem *Ulysses* (Aldington, 1967). Towards the end of the poem, Ulysses is talking with a group of his old traveling friends, and says:

How dull it is to pause, to make an end. To rust unburnished, not to shine in use! Old age has yet his honor and his toil. Death closes all; but something ere the end, Some word of noble note, may yet be done (p. 863).

Ulysses then summons his comrades:

Come my friends,
'Tis not too late to seek a newer world.'

And he goes on to say:

Tho' much is taken, much abides; and tho'
We are not now that strength which in old days
Moved earth and heaven; that which we are, we are;
One equal temper of heroic hearts,
Made weak by time and fate, but strong in will
To strive, to seek, to find, and not to yield (p. 864).

Those of us who are working in the field with aging individuals recognize the great number of opportunities there are to help people "to strive, to seek, to find, and not to yield, " in their search for self-fulfillment in their later years. In fact, there is no facet of human behavior which holds greater potential for abundant living than does the "re-creative" use of leisure. Yet, there is perhaps no other facet that is less understood, or more underrated.

This is the concept by which I base my thoughts about recreation as an opportunity for people to express themselves through their leisure in order that they might truly experience the art of living. According to Dr. George Romney (1965):

> Recreation's purpose is not to kill time but rather to make time live; not to help the individual serve time, but to make time serve the individual; not to encourage people to hide from themselves, but to help them find themselves. . . (p. 122).

With these words written over 36 years ago, Dr. Romney added to the foundations of "recreation as an expression"—an expression of the "re-creation" of goals towards a sense of individual fulfillment. We realize that expression means feeling, spirit, character—and conveys a thought, an attitude, a movement toward some kind of action.

In all lifestyles, I would suggest that recreation is indeed "re-creation," an act of creating anew, a time for refreshment of the body and the mind, the creative adventure of living as a "Ulyssean" adult. (McLeish, 1976).

Peterson (1968) speaks of the art of living as truly the art of the "adventure" of living:

> A man practices the art of adventure when he heroically faces up to life; when he has the daring to open doors to new experiences and to step boldly forth to explore new horizons; when he breaks the chain of routine and renews his life through reading new books, traveling to new places, making new friends, taking up new hobbies, and adopting new viewpoints; when he recognizes that the only ceiling life has is the one he gives it and comes to realize that he is surrounded by infinite possibilities for growth and achievement; when he concludes that a rut is only another name for a grave and the only way to stay out of ruts is by living adventurously and staying vitally alive every day of his life.

In his book, *The Human Use of Human Beings*, Weiner (1954) notes: "Any use of a human being, in which less is demanded of him and less is attributed to him than his full status, is a degradation and a waste." (p. 72)

Let us not continue to degrade or lay to waste one of our nation's greatest natural resources: our older adults. By now we're all aware of the statistics relating to the over sixty-five generation, whose numbers are more than 26 million at this time, and are expected to double by the year 2010. The "baby boom" of the 1940s is indeed having an impact on the demographics of the future. Also, a slightly increasing life expectancy is indicated.

Compulsory retirement, elongation of the expected lifespan, reduction of work opportunities, loss of social status and contacts because of withdrawal from jobs, difficult housing conditions, lessened financial wherewithal, and little preparation for fulfilling use of leisure time—all combine to produce a large population of *potentially* distressed and lonely people, owning a large number of discretionary hours. What opportunities they have in their "non-work" time may help either to provide important social/psychological adjustments or may condemn them to an elongated period of "graveyard-watching." Rusk (1960) makes the wise observation: "We are now in the position of curing many diseases and helping people stay well, only to see many drop back into illness through the malignancy of idleness."

Our elderly population has become the significant most tragically alienated, disadvantaged, and disserviced segment of American society. Despite legislation against mandatory retirement, millions of vigorous, talented, experienced persons are still forced into retirement at the peak of their productivity, and at a time when the community can truly make valuable use of their knowledge, skills, and experiences. Unfortunately, many older people are themselves convinced that they are no longer of value—either to themselves, or to society. Sadly, the stereotypes of aging often become self-fulfilling prophesies—reinforced by society's attitudes and actions.

However, it is through leisure endeavors that people can come to recognize their potentials and to develop options for a sense of self-fulfillment—to experience the "Ulyssean" adventure of living.

Scientists tell us that we as individuals realize only about 5 percent of our potentials in a lifetime—only about 15 percent of our brain power. Just imagine what potentials there are that exist below the surface of this giant iceburg, the human potential. It should be the task, and the challenge, of each and every one of us to help others,

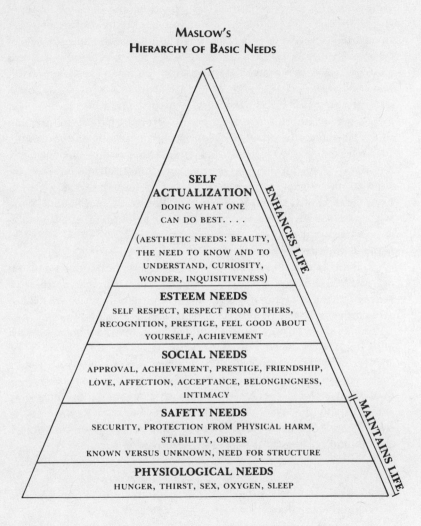

MASLOW'S
HIERARCHY OF BASIC NEEDS

SELF ACTUALIZATION
DOING WHAT ONE CAN DO BEST. . . .

(AESTHETIC NEEDS: BEAUTY, THE NEED TO KNOW AND TO UNDERSTAND, CURIOSITY, WONDER, INQUISITIVENESS)

ESTEEM NEEDS
SELF RESPECT, RESPECT FROM OTHERS, RECOGNITION, PRESTIGE, FEEL GOOD ABOUT YOURSELF, ACHIEVEMENT

SOCIAL NEEDS
APPROVAL, ACHIEVEMENT, PRESTIGE, FRIENDSHIP, LOVE, AFFECTION, ACCEPTANCE, BELONGINGNESS, INTIMACY

SAFETY NEEDS
SECURITY, PROTECTION FROM PHYSICAL HARM, STABILITY, ORDER
KNOWN VERSUS UNKNOWN, NEED FOR STRUCTURE

PHYSIOLOGICAL NEEDS
HUNGER, THIRST, SEX, OXYGEN, SLEEP

ENHANCES LIFE

MAINTAINS LIFE

through recreational endeavors, to identify their potentials and to develop viable options—"to strive, to seek, to find, and not to yield."

Maslow (1970), the humanistic psychologist was convinced that "the man will strive towards self-actualization once the lower levels of needs are met" (p. 38). Much of our work in the field of gerontology is directed towards helping individuals fulfill just the lowest levels of Maslow's hierarchy of human needs: the physiological needs (hunger, thirst, sex, oxygen, sleep), and the safety needs (security, protection from physical harm, stability, order, knowing vs. unknowing, structure). These are the needs which *maintain* life.

Once those needs are cared for, however, we can begin directing our attention to the other levels of needs, significant in our striving for self-actualization: the social needs (approval, achievement, prestige, friendship, love, affection, acceptance, belongingness, intimacy), the esteem needs (self-respect, respect from others, recognition, feeling good about oneself), and finally, self-actualization (doing what one can do best, aesthetic needs, the need to know and to understand, curiosity, wonder, inquisitiveness). Maslow identifies these as the needs which *enhance* life.

As we work with retired persons, we realize the significance that recreational activities can play in an individual's struggle to achieve a sense of value. It is important for those of us who work in the field to realize that *whatever* the retired person does, the activity or involvement *must* have meaning and some degree of reward associated with it. That reward need not be measured by dollars, but may be measured by the person's sense of achievement, recognition, and/or the "legitimacy" of that activity. These rewards can be just as valuable as dollars. Because the over sixty-five generation represents such a widely diverse social group, appropriate recreational services must include a wide variety of opportunities—opportunities which, according to Moran (1979), include the following:

1. Afford status, recognition, and achievement;
2. Provide a social group as a replacement for former co-workers and companions;
3. Include a variety of interests directly related to adjustments being experienced;
4. Develop positive attitudes toward leisure pursuits;
5. Provide meaningful expression to self and others, or are

creative in terms of both traditional and contemporary social values;

6. Contain aspects of work. This is especially important for the individual whose life previously focused on work-related activities. This would include hobbies which are useful or can be sold.

7. Are recurrent, organized, visible to a social audience, permit a range of participation, and foster the formation of new roles.

And I would like to add an eighth standard:

8. Establish an environment conducive and non-threatening to the individual's experimenting with new ideas and testing possible new endeavors—an environment especially supportive for individual's taking realistic risks to achieve self-fulfillment.

I have recently become especially interested in helping aging persons to take "reasonable" risks. (By the way, my reference to the term "aging persons" includes those of us who are in our middle years!) Like growing, risk-taking is concerned with giving up false beliefs, compromised allegiances, misdirected investments, superficial attachments and destructive habits, according to Viscott. Should a person postpone taking reasonable risks, the time eventually comes when he or she will either be forced to accept a situation that he or she doesn't like, or made to take a risk totally unprepared. If one continues to shun *any* risk, one is more than likely to become comfortable with fewer and fewer experiences. The world shrinks, and so with it, the individual can become rigid and withdrawn.

Viscott provides us with a proverb:

If you cannot risk, you cannot grow,
If you cannot grow, you cannot become your best,
If you cannot become your best, you cannot be happy.
If you cannot be happy, what else matters?

We know Maslow suggests that the ultimate human need is for "self-actualization," a need which involves personal risk-taking. The self-actualized person creates action where there otherwise would be none, and provides the fuel for most business, professional, and cultural endeavors. This is the person who is "growth-oriented" and is willing to take risks.

Out of each new experience comes a sense of change. From each change can come a sense of growth. And from growth we experience development. . .which creates the willingness to change, to grow, to develop. A continuous, dynamic, and exciting pattern evolves:

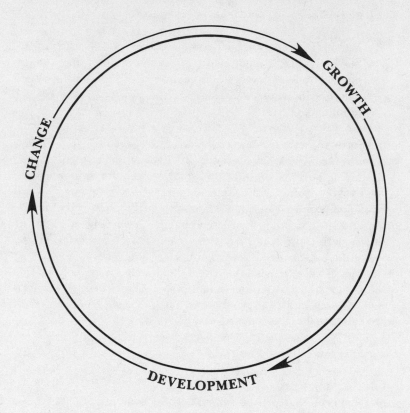

Still, there are two very real obstacles to growth, according to Maslow (1968): 1) the refusal to treat anything with deep seriousness, concern and commitment; and 2) the refusal to try to realize one's full potentials (p. 342).

We are content with the security of the known rather than the challenge of the new. . .though in principle, self-actualization is easy, in practice, it rarely happens. In fact, only about one percent of the adult population reach their full potential in a lifetime! (p. 204).

(Most writers say about 5 percent of the adult population reach their full potential in a lifetime—Maslow allows for a mere 1 percent!)

From my perspective, a risk-taker generally recognizes the importance of realistic expectations, sound planning, and the condition that one takes no *unnecessary* risks. This person is a logical thinker who considers all available facts before making a decision. Moreover, his or her action steps involve the mental processes concerned with forming conclusions, judgments, or inferences. These processes lead to sound decisions based upon a well thought-out exploration of a problem.

Why do we avoid risks? It is generally because of a fear of failure itself or a fear of the embarrassment we may experience because of a failure. Remember, the only people who never make mistakes are those who never do anything. For too long, ''risk'' has been defined in terms of hazards or dangerous endeavors. Perhaps it is time to view the taking of risks as an opportunity for personal growth—as a daring adventure.

Just as in Tennyson's *Ulysses,* the ''Ulyssean'' adult knows that advancing years do bring on possible hazards. They recognize that some of their physical powers have diminished. But they seem to take hold of their life, and do not appear to fret about such declines and deficits, knowing, as did Ulysses, that there is still an abundance of power remaining, which with careful planning and use, will serve them well. Ulyssean adults are past masters at risk-taking.

Several years ago, I was asked to participate in a one-half hour documentary on the Senior Olympics. As my husband and I arrived at the stadium we heard a great roar go up from the crowd in the stadium. We hurried out onto the track area to see what was happening. Volunteers were stretching ribbon across the finish line in preparation for an event finish. The crowd rose to their feet and cheered. We looked down on the track and there on the outside lane, finishing the 6 1/2 mile walk, was a sight I shall always remember. A woman, about 4 feet and 10 inches tall, in a cotton frock hanging to her mid-calves, tennis shoes and floppy bobby-socks, with a wide brimmed straw hat, walking at a good pace and Hulda Crooks was finishing her event—at eighty-one years of age.

We talked with Hulda after she received her gold medal, and found that she had participated in many exciting challenges in her life: one being that in August of that year she would be making her sixteenth annual climb of Mt. Whitney. A truly "Ulyssean" adult!

Think for a moment how the events in history have affected the decisions you've made at various milestones in your own lifetime—or how those events may even affect the decisions you'll make in the future. What was happening in history when you were born?—entering or completing various educational levels?—First job?—Job changes?—Marriage?—Children arriving, growing up, leaving home? What events in history have had an impact upon how you have or haven't acted? How have historical happenings affected your major life decisions—your lifestyle and value system?

Think about older persons and the tremendous changes that have occurred across their lifespans—and what effect these changes have had upon their values, philosophies, and decisions. I am struck by the analogy between time and the metronome. The metronome provides an interesting demonstration of a concept of time. For instance, when we are twelve years of age, the metronome of time seems to go at its slowest pace, waiting to be thirteen, entering that desired time called the "teens!"

When does time go very slowly for us? When we are waiting for an important event? When we're pregnant? When we're ill, or are recovering from an illness? When we are lonely? As we grow older, however, many of us find that time seems to pass much too quickly. When does time seem to go much too fast for us? When we are having fun? As we get older? Summer vacations? When a task has to be completed?

There is another time in our lives during which time could go very slowly—retirement. Retirement is certainly a major transition period during which we may suddenly have to consider what we are doing with our time. Some look upon this point in time as did George Bernard Shaw who wrote: "A perpetual holiday is just another definition of hell". Others, however, look upon it as a "gift"—a gift of time.

Let's look at the word retirement. The dictionary defines it as: falling backward. . .retreating in an orderly fashion and according to plan, as from battle or untenable position. . .to fall back from danger. . .to withdraw a machine permanently from its role of service, usually for scrapping. . .going to bed!

Surely, there is a need to change these more historical definitions of the word. I propose that we start a movement to persuade editors and publishers of dictionaries across the nation to review the definition of "retirement," and ask that they provide a meaning more in keeping with today's concept. . .a time for freedom. . .a time for renewal. . .a time for "re-creation". . .a time for the adventure of living.

Retirement is sometimes perceived as a crisis. The Chinese language provides an intriguing calligraphy for the word "crisis." There are two characters represented in this calligraphy. The upper character represents "danger," and the lower means "opportunity." In the character for "danger," there are very few strokes, whereas in the character for "opportunity," there are many more strokes. . .an observation which could indicate that there are many more opportunities in a crisis than there are dangers.

TRANSLATION: CRISIS

We have many perceptions of retirement. Perceptions which color our conscious and unconscious efforts to plan for and live within this period of life.

196   VALUES, ETHICS AND AGING

Historically, retirement has often conjured up fears in the minds of many people—concerns about failing health, loneliness, a lack of self-worth, and financial security. A reality about retirement, however, is the *time* we inherit with this major life transition. I would like you to have to use your imagination with me for the next few minutes:

> Standing before you today is the great Wizard of Time. This great wizard has a gift for you, a gift of 24 hours. Twenty-four hours over which you have complete control, and you may do with them as you wish. What will you do with this gift of time?

> Now, let's look into the future. Years have passed by. Just a few years for some—many years for others. You are now ready to retire. The great Wizard of Time appears before you once again with another gift to bestow upon you. This time it is a gift of 35,000 hours! The wizard is giving you 35,000 hours over which you have complete control—you can determine how these hours will serve YOU. These hours represent the time you formerly devoted to full-time work, 5 days a week, 8 hours each work day, and don't even include evening and weekend hours!

National statistics indicate that we can plan on an average of 15 years in active retirement. You've been working about 8 hours a day for many years. Upon retirement, those work hours will be translated into 35,000 hours of discretionary time—time for "re-creation." What we do with this gift of time may very well determine our mental and physical vitality throughout our later years.

A clever poem by Arnold related:

> He is miserable and wretched
> And ignorant too,
> Who has nothing to do,
> When he has nothing to do.

> He is rich and happy,
> And fortunate too,

Who has plenty to do,
When he has nothing to do!

Most people plan relatively well for their financial circumstances
in retirement, for where they want to live, for how to maintain health
and vitality, or for some of the legal issues which must be resolved.
But, what about the recreative use of this gift of time? Unfortunately,
very little consideration is given to those 35,000 hours we inherit with
retirement.

Research indicates that in retirement, we are very likely (given
reasonably good health) to be engaged in some of those very same interests and activities we have developed over a lifespan. Some experts
(Maddox, 1968) have proposed that there is a "persistence of life style"
(181) among the retired. A number of studies indicate that how an
older person uses his or her leisure depends to a large degree upon the
skills and interests developed when he or she was young.

Neugarten (1968) proposed that the individual develops habits,
associations, commitments, preferences, and a host of other factors
which become his or her personality. As a person ages, he or she is in-
clined to maintain a continuity—a persistence of such factors. The individual's lifelong experiences create certain predispositions which
one will continue to maintain. This approach indicates that change
and adaptation are continuous throughout the life cycle and involve
interaction among all of the elements of influence upon the individual
(p. 177). Remember the change cycle? Change. . .Growth. . .
Development. . .?

Havighurst (1961), reporting on some data from his Kansas City
studies, indicates that the more interests in which an individual is involved in retirement, the more likely he or she will have a higher
degree of life satisfaction in retirement. There may be a point of no
return, however, when we are so involved in so many activities that
we achieve no sense of life satisfaction. Also, experience indicates that
the more diversified are the individual's interests, the higher is the
reported level of life satisfaction (p. 173).

Research and field experience both suggest that there are strong
benefits to be recognized from early planning for the numerous
possibilities that exist for achieving a sense of self-fulfillment in retirement. However, most of us need some guidance in exploring those
possibilities. It is through careful analysis of one's skills, knowledge,

and experience that we are able to determine appropriate directions in planning for a sense of life satisfaction as we continue our aging process.

Research continues to support the need for sound planning. In a Harris poll study (1975), *The Myths of Aging*, retired subjects were asked: "If you had it to do over again, what would you have done differently in planning for your retirement?" The overriding response was: "I would have started planning much earlier in my life" (p. 34). The retired are indeed sending very strong messages back to those of us who have not yet retired. Will we take their advice or will we be making the same kind of statement to others when we have retired?

It should be noted that if we have developed diverse interests prior to retirement, we are likely to be able to adapt more successfully to the changes that may occur in retirement. However, there is one pervasive stereotype we must destroy: that older people cannot learn new things, or develop new skills without a tremendous effort. Not so! It may take us a little longer to learn, but we can learn just as well as younger people. The following example will emphasize the concept of the adventure of a new experience, a sense of personal achievement, and a demonstration of recreation as expression:

I have a friend whose daughter called her one day in tears. The daughter explained, "Mother, do you remember the doll you played with—you know, the one you gave to me as a child to play with—your old doll—the doll I wanted Sue Ann to play with too? I felt it was time to give it to her and went up to the attic to dig it out of the storage box. I found it all chewed up and in pieces. The mice got at it, I guess. I'm so upset and don't know what to do about it. Only the head is in one piece; the cotton body is almost totally destroyed. I'm sick!"

My friend told her daughter that she would pick it up and see what she could do with it. There is a doll hospital not too far from her, and she decided to take the remains there for advice. At the doll hospital, she became very interested in how dolls were put back together again. She asked the owner if she could learn how to mend dolls, and if she could just volunteer to help and thus learn. The owner was delighted to have this offer of help as she had a large back-order list and could not even accept any more dolls until she had caught up.

My friend became so interested in her new hobby that she checked out books on the subject of old dolls and doll restoration. She developed a fine skill and took up doll-mending as a serious endeavor. After reading many books, going to doll and antique shows, "interning" at the doll hospital, and talking with others involved in this hobby, she emerged as an expert in restoring old dolls. She became so proficient and knowledgeable that she began to charge for her services. She started to write articles and to participate in fairs, exhibitions and special doll shows. She began to teach others and was even earning a small supplementary income from her "hobby"—enough to pay for her expenses. By this time, she had gained national recognition for her expertise and was sought after to talk before groups. By the way, she is seventy-five years of age. Indeed, she is one of those "Ulyssean" adults to whom I have referred several times.

My friend has been meeting new people and expanding her options. She had identified a potential she did not know she had. Her life has new meaning, a new sense of value and achievement. She has drawn upon a new interest and has trained herself to be an expert at her new skill. Certainly, from many perspectives, she is using her time effectively and in many rewarding ways—to herself and to others.

Unfortunately, many people are never exposed to the positive elements of worthwhile leisure or to the development of rewarding recreational endeavors. Some people may have more time on their hands than they have the knowledge, the interest and/or the curiosity to handle. Many have become so conditioned to passive leisure forms that they have forgotten how to motivate or to amuse themselves—they have either forgotten the art of living—or never even experienced it. Many people live vicariously through the actions of others and the possession of things.

DeGrazia (1964) in his masterful study on *Time, Work and Leisure,* observed: "The individual seems free. . .but he is buffeted by advertising and dazed by winking lights and bright colors as if he were a rustic. The more he spends to save time and buy status, the more he must work to have the money to save time!" (p. 213).

In fact, recently I saw a cartoon picturing a man standing in front of a garage with his wife standing nearby. She has a camera and is taking a picture of him. He is posing, with pride, before his garage and driveway filled with possessions. In the cartoon we can see a boat, a trailer, a snowmobile, a sports car, bicycles, woodworking equipment, water skiis, a golf bag, snow skiis, a Ping-Pong table, two motorcyles, and tennis rackets on the wall. The caption under the cartoon read: "Hurry up and take the picture! I've got to get back to work!" Back to work. With very little time allotted to using any of these products of the "affluent society."

In my work with middle aged persons, I find many who are in this very same predicament, having many recreational and leisure possessions, but not willing to allot the time truly to enjoy the values inherent not only in the possessions themselves, but more importantly, in the "recreative" challenge these possessions represent. Will these people be able to look upon their inheritance of 35,000 hours in retirement as a gift or as a burden? Will they be able to look upon recreation as an expression? As an expression of the art of living?

Indeed, the art of living knows no limits by age or physical ability, as illustrated by the earlier example with regard to my participation in the Senior Olympics. It proved to be a memorable day for several reasons, the most exciting being the introduction to our hiking friend, Hulda Crooks. A second reason was our introduction to another "Ulyssean" adult. About 2 hours after our arrival, we heard a great roar go up again from those in the stands at the stadium. We noticed that volunteers were putting up the ribbon across the track for an event's ending, and we rushed to the edge of the track to see what was happening. As I looked up to the far turn of the track, I saw a vision I shall never forget, for there was a gentleman on his last few yards of the 6 1/2 mile walk event—finishing it hours after the last participant had crossed the line—finishing this event with a hand cane in each hand and a leg brace on each leg.

Yes, indeed, "come my friends, 'tis not too late to seek a newer world; though much is taken, much abides" (Aldington, 1967). Here are a few suggestions that can help us experience the true adventure of living:

1. Renew energy! (Recognize enthusiasm as a source of energy).
2. Resist laziness! (Take risks, with reason).
3. Avoid procrastination!
4. Banish boredom!
5. Seek balance! (Stretch the body, the mind and the self!)
6. Explore new ideas!

7. Dream dreams!
8. Set goals!
9. Take action!

In Tennyson's words (Aldington, 1967), the challenge should be:

". . .strong in will
To strive, to seek, to find, and not to yield" (p. 964).

REFERENCES

Aldington, Richard. *The Viking Book of Poetry of the English-Speaking World.* "Ulysses" (by Alfred Tennyson). New York: The Viking Press, 1967.

Boyack, V.L. *Women in their middle years.* Unpublished dissertation, University of Southern California, 1977.

DeGrazia, S. *Of time, work and leisure.* Garden City, N.Y.: Doubleday & Co., Anchor Books, 1964.

Goals for American Recreation. Washington, D.C.: American Association of Health, Physical Education and Recreation, 1964.

Havighurst, R.J. The nature and values of meaningful free-time activity. In R.W. Kleemeir (Ed.) *Aging and leisure: A research perspective into the meaningful use of time.* New York: Oxford University Press, 1961.

Louis Harris & Associates. *The myth and reality of aging in America.* Washington, D.C.: National Council on the Aging, Inc. 1975.

Maddox, G.L. Persistence of life style among the elderly: A longitudinal study of patterns of social activity in relation to life satisfaction. In B.L. Neurgarten (Ed.) *Middle age and aging: A reader in social psychology.* Chicago: University of Chicago Press, 1968.

Maslow, A.H. *Toward a Psychology of Being.* Princeton, New Jersey: Van Nostrand & Reinhold, 1968.

Maslow, A.H. *Motivation and personality, (2nd ed.)* New York: Harper & Row, 1970.

McLeish, J.A.B. *The Ulyssean adult: Creativity in the middle and later years.* Toronto, Canada: McGraw-Hill Ryerson Limited, 1976.

Neugarten, B.L. (Ed.). *Middle age and aging: A reader in social psychology*. Chicago: University of Chicago Press, 1968.

Peterson, W. *More about the art of living*. Simon & Schuster, 1968.

Rusk, H.M.D., *Therapeutic recreation: Hospital management*, April 1960. LXXIZ, 4.

Weiner, N. *The Human Use of Human Beings: Cybernetics and Society*. New York: Avon Books, 1954.

INDEX

DATE DUE